The Friends of St. Francis

THE FRIENDS
OF ST. FRANCIS

by

Sidney F. Wicks

*"So you are the man everybody is fussing about?
You had better see that you make good, or you
are going to have something to answer for."*
— *Admonition of a rustic to
the mystic St. Francis*

FRANCISCAN HERALD PRESS
CHICAGO, ILLINOIS 1952

Nihil obstat: Conradin Wallbraun O.F.M., Censor Librorum
Imprimi potest: Eligius Weir O.F.M., Minister Provincial
Imprimatur: +Samuel Cardinal Stritch, Archiepiscopus Chica-
giensis May 9, 1952

Foreword

THERE ARE so many books written about the subject of St. Francis of Assisi. Why add another one? Sabatier wrote what people with his viewpoint call the classic volume, and G. K. Chesterton wrote the brilliant treatise. Can any new fact be unearthed, anything fresh said? But yes, indeed! For the authentic sign of a saint lies in his power to quicken souls in each succeeding generation. Every new soul that is lit by his spirit and subdued by his compassion has just that one surprising fact to reveal, that fresh testimony to make. Something new is learned about St. Francis from every man who surrenders his heart to him. Every young man who falls in love believes that he perceives a truth and a beauty none ever saw before. That is his excuse for writing a sonnet. It is my excuse for writing this book.

I had no deliberate intention of writing it. But my honored friend Father Declan Flynn O.F.M., editor of *The Franciscan,* asked me to write a series of ar-

ticles about St. Francis. There followed requests from
The Franciscan Review of Montreal and from *The
Franciscan Herald and Forum* of Chicago. Thus, I
accumulated much Franciscan material; and the relevance of the Third Order to the world's problem today began to weigh on me.

At least, I thought, it should be interesting to show
how St. Francis had come to inspire a man who is
not primarily a literary man but one deeply immersed
in the social activities of England's industrial North
and who has lived a long professional and business
life. To me St. Francis is not a literary theme, a
curiosity for biographers, a romantic story. Assisi is
not the Lake District with its Wordsworthian Pilgrims.
St. Francis is a living power among all sorts and conditions of men, quickening them to a new way of
life, illuminating the social problems that bewilder
them. Therefore, this book is a confession of faith,
an evidence, as it were, of the reaction of one who
("Too late have I loved thee") was received into the
Catholic Church only a few years ago, and who still
treasures the affection of his many Protestant friends.

The timeless vitality of St. Francis is revealed in his
power of making friends with unlikely people. He is
always shaking hands with a wolf in some new
Gubbio. Free Churchmen are not wolves, even in
sheep's clothing, but somehow St. Francis has become
a kind of patron saint to Non-conformists. They have

the same affection for him as they have for the gentle
monk Thomas a Kempis of the *Imitatio Christi*. But
while Thomas a Kempis whispered from his cell, St.
Francis speaks with a singing voice in the open air, a
living aggressive evangelist. St. Francis does not pro-
voke theological controversy or challenge the intellect with any Thomist philosophy—he whole-heart-
edly accepted the faith and discipline of his Church.
It is his utter simplicity, his flaming compassion, his
love of the common folk, his adoration of the bright
and breathing world of trees and buds and flowers,
that break down prejudice. It was indeed the super-
intendent of a Congregational Sunday school who
first introduced me to St. Francis by his habit of telling us children thrilling stories of the saint's adven-
tures. In consequence, I bought a copy with hard
earned shillings of Canton's *Child's Book of Saints*.
I was a young and ardent Non-conformist who wrote
to the local papers attacking High Church curates for
their Papist practices. One of them poured coals of
fire on my head—in the spirit of St. Francis—by giving
me a pocket volume of Robert Browning's poems. I
liked saints, but never dreamed that I should ever ask
them to pray for me. St. Francis was a fine romantic
fellow, but I did not know that one day he would
speak to me from the eternal places. At least this
book affords me the opportunity of paying tribute to
the old minister of my chapel who preached sermons

inspired by Watts's "When I Survey the Wondrous Cross."

I trust this book is free from any taint of propaganda. There is nothing in it but a simple desire to pay tribute to a saint who has done so much for me. If there is any propaganda in it, it is certainly not directed to my Protestant friends, but to my fellow Catholics. I would humbly remind them that time and again when the fires of the Church burnt low, a saint has emerged to rekindle the fire of God's love. The Church is revivified not by outward attacks, but by inner revival. This recurrent revival is the mission of the saints. But it is the Church which breeds the saints, not the critical world. May the spirit of St. Francis inspire us all with a new compassion for our fellow men throughout the world, a new desire for the universal Peace of God, a new resolution to rebuild the world on the justice and the mercy of God; a new prayer that Christ may reconcile mankind to his Father; a new faith amid economic perplexities that if we first seek the kingdom of God and his justice, all the things we need will be added unto us. If we have the spirit of St. Francis, we shall count ourselves rich and we shall ask for nothing more.

SIDNEY F. WICKS,

Easter Sunday, 1951.

Contents

Part I

The Traits of St. Francis

CHAPTER 1

The Complexity of St. Francis

THE WEAKNESS of contemporary Christianity is its over-simplification of the personality of our Blessed Lord. Jesus is pictured as a poet among the lilies of Galilee. Some hymn writers do for Galilee what the worshippers of Wordsworth did for the Lake District. I have read poems which made play with the moonlight shining through the olive trees of Gethsemane. The truth lies not so much in a simple Jesus as in an enigmatic Christ.

Simplification is an escape from hard thinking: we prefer a cradle to a creed. The old Adam likes to lull the soul with a Savior who mooned among the lilies of the field, meditated by the blue waters of Galilee, smiled at little children. In the tremendous sentence "Lamb of God who takest away the sins of the World," it is the lamb which the mind fondles. We compose a sonnet to a little white lamb and shun the dark and dreadful mystery of the Cross. Thus in our craving for simplicity we shun the enormous complexity of the Incarnation and the Redemption.

And just in that way St. Francis has been treated. The happy-hearted humanitarian simplifies him into a gay truant who ran away from a pagan school for a picnic in green pastures and by still waters. A troubadour of God! A singer of songs! To the dark complexity of the problem of his stigmata we are blind. His love of flowers and birds and beasts we smile at as an amiable foible and as one smiles at an old maid who loves cats. But St. Francis did not pamper pet pomeranians or croon to a canary. It takes more hardihood to shake hands with a wolf! But precisely what he loved were "creatures" of God, children of the creative love which broke forth in a singing lark and a dying Lord. To him birds and flowers and sun and moon were not trinkets, they were sacraments. And if St. Francis walked in a dew-filled garden on a prosperous morn in May, it was because he made a complex synthesis of the Garden of Eden and the Garden of Gethsemane. He knew both, and no man more than he.

Study his characteristic gesture. It was stripping something off. He began by stripping off his father's coat of many colors and ended by dying naked on the ground. The soul of man is not like Peer Gynt's onion, from which one strips off layer after layer until one comes to—nothing! Man is created with

the indestructible core of the soul and begins immediately to put on swathe after swathe of garments—
self-love, pride, greed, lust, love of honor and wealth,
until he is completely dressed in a little brief authority. To strip off the accumulated wardrobe of sin
is not a simple matter nor is the man who essays
it a simpleton. In our hearts we regard a simple man
as a simpleton. But the simple man is he who has
so unraveled the complex tangle of truth that his
solution looks simple. Is it simple? Try stripping
off only one habit and see! St. Francis stripped off
every one, and at last died naked with the Stigmata
on his hands. A very complex person!

To become followers of St. Francis we need to
be more than simple romantics, smiling humanitarians. It is better to start with the Nicene creed,
better to discover the truth that

"Praestet Fides supplementum
Sensuum defectui."

St. Francis originated the making of a crib at
Christmastide. Who does not feel the glamor of
the picture of the gracious Lady bending over her
Babe in a manger, the ox and the ass standing by
and shepherds adoring? But to St. Francis the crib
was the child's picture book of the tremendous
complexity of the Incarnation and of how Mary
could be Mater Dei.

This complex saint calls us to journey towards an ultimate simplicity, and strait and narrow is the road.

CHAPTER 2

The Coming of a Saint

THE MOTHER of Saint Francis gave the name of John to her son. His father, a typically bold and adventurous merchant of his day, was traveling in France at the time. On his return he renamed the babe Francesco, thus giving evidence of a strong admiration for Italy's sister country. This link with the fructifying traditions and culture of France, which has given so many saints to Holy Church, is interesting to those who still feel a deep stirring of pride when they remember the motherland of their forefathers. Italian by birth, French by name, English by love's adoption, Saint Francis does not so much provide a link between great peoples as unify them in a common impulse of reverence. The fact that his father, a wholesale cloth merchant, was so adventurously abroad at the time of his birth is significant of the growing economic freedom of the times. But while the father of Francis went for custom and its gold, the spirit of Saint Francis went for Christ and his glory.

Whenever God almighty, the Father omnipotent,

has willed to reveal himself, he has not appeared in a dramatic apocalypse. That magnificent and sonorous Latin hymn, the Dies Irae, does indeed picture the Last Day as a lurid dawn heralded by

"Tuba mirum spargens sonum
Per sepulchra regionum."

But this is not consonant with the analogies which history provides. Who would dare to speculate—but it is possible when the last day dawns we shall wake intensely expectant and aware, gazing at our souls with lucid apprehension and hearing against the rose and silver of the eastern sky, poignant and piercing sweet, the song of the bird.

Before the Nativity the minds of men were dark with the cark and cancer of despair, the bitter fruit of the ineradicable bias of sin without a Savior. Morbid dreams, lurid prophecies, as well as the prayer-born hope and desire of the faithful readers of the Scriptures, bred expectations of a Messiah. It would have been in keeping with the military splendor of the Roman legions; with the vulgar and flaunting gladiatorial shows, where the blood of hired men welled into the sand amid trumpets and cheers; with the glittering vice and violence of imperial Rome, and with the proletarian belief in the politics of power, if the Messiah had come with thunder and lightning on the clouds, an apocalypse of dazzling angelic hosts.

He did not so come. There was a maiden with a face like a rose and a heart like a lily who felt beneath her heart the faint stirrings of a little life and who in whispers rehearsed a lullaby. So the Lord Christ came.

What of the world in which the babe Francesco was born? Was there apocalyptic expectancy? Certainly there was expectancy, vague yet intoxicating. Most men felt that stir which we feel within our unconscious deeps when roots long buried in winter first thrill with the pang and apprehension of spring. But others experienced the nervous tension which presages the thunderstorm. The souls of men were dimly aware that the iron penance for the deadly poisonous sins of paganism by which the Church saved civilization, yet so as by fire, was loosening its manacles and that they were free to try a more adventurous liberty of life. The frame of society was shaken by new economic forces of which the newly rich merchant was a symbol. The toilers were heaving their shoulders against feudal serfdom. Gaiety, festive though forced, broke out in lute, viol and song. There was violent sin and splendid repentance, emotional instability, exuberance without purpose. For five years, severe dearth preceded the birth of Francis, and this would enhance the contrasts of the age.

What then should men expect? A knight errant, splendid in plume and armor, invincible in the lists?

A ringing denunciation of wrong, breaking all
shackles and vows and thundering on church doors
with a dogmatic hammer? Somebody, surely, as
gaudy and dramatic and vivid and violent as the age?
Anything might happen in a world like that. What
happened was St. Francis; and men heard in the dark
of the dawn—a song!

They heard the melody of the Pied Piper of
Umbria.

They saw a man with ragged habit and singing
voice who scraped two sticks together in childlike imi-
tation of a fiddle and called flowers and rivers and
birds his brothers and sisters. Not a magnificent man,
not a leader of a magniloquent movement—but a
Little Poor Man. That is how St. Francis came.
Gilbert Keith Chesterton wrote: "While it was yet
twilight a figure appeared silently and suddenly on
a little hill above the city, dark against the fading
darkness. For it was the end of a long and stern
night, a night of vigil, not unvisited by stars. He
stood with his hands uplifted, as in so many statues
and pictures, and about him was a burst of birds
singing; and behind him was the break of day."

I have written
          "not a magnificent man,
           not a magniloquent movement."
In these days when movements take precedence over
men, and ideologies are idols, and societies are

saviors, and councils are consecrate, the truth that St. Francis came forth as an individual representing only the single impulse of a single soul, needs to be studied and stressed. Indeed St. Francis defined individualism with literal accuracy. When he saw a church in ruins, he did not convene a committee, but carried stones: he did not lobby for a proposed and seconded resolution by show of hands, but resolved to build the walls with his own bare hands. He organized no union of workers in the Lord's vineyard; he labored in a vineyard when he needed a crust. He did not form a missionary society for the conversion of Saracens; he risked his life and went and preached to the Sultan.

When of its own accord the multitude flocked to him, so that this work looked like a movement, he became bewildered; and when a directive body became imperative for such a movement, he might well have become a man of sorrows. Prevalent undisciplined liberty turning into license was a source of grave anxiety to the Church. There were already enthusiasts enough, the Umiliati, the Cathari and the Poor Men of Lyons, pacifist and critical of the Church. If St. Francis had begun by sitting down and drawing up the rules of a new movement, one can imagine that the patient and worried Pope Innocent would have heaved a sigh and muttered "What, another?" By the grace of God St. Francis was as incapable of

drawing up the charter regulations of a movement as
a skylark is incapable of composing a Beethoven sym-
phony. Both St. Francis and the skylark sang, as
Wordsworth wrote, "in profuse strains of unpremedi-
tated art."

CHAPTER 3

The Troubadour of God

CHAPTER ONE might well have been called "The Contradictions of St. Francis." We call him the troubadour of God—and even le jongleur de Dieu— but at La Verna of the Apennines a vision of glorified sorrow left the nail-prints of the Cross on his hands and feet. He chanted a great song on lordly Brother Sun, but made a retreat in a dark cavern; he praised the joyfulness of Brother Fire, but welcomed the pain of frozen snow; he was courteous to Brother Wolf, but harsh to Brother Ass (as he called his body); he cried out in lyric rapture at Mother Earth and the abundance of flowers and fruits, but he says "Be praised, O God, of our brother Death of Body."

Great men are men of enormous contradictions. But a saint is more complex than the great man. He is a man who is living a supernatural life. He must needs be a man of complexity and contradiction, for he is essaying in his life the synthesis of the Incarnation and the Cross. He says that the King of Kings is "so sweet and small" in the cradle of Bethlehem, and then tells us that those baby hands scattered the morning stars in the firmament and were at last nailed to a tree.

One of the contradictions in St. Francis is a matter of great need to Christendom in these days of gloom. I refer to the gaiety of St. Francis. I dream of a new generation of Franciscans (I am thinking only of the Third Order) who will live among their fellows in an astonishing gaiety of manner and mood. Dare I say I have sensed among those who were given the privilege of being born on the knees of Mother Church a certain close-lipped reticence? But today St. Francis is singing again. It were good if the Church's praise were to overflow her walls and to ring among the poor peripatetic prodigals without. The stricken world needs a new laughter. The sophisticated laughter, which is "as the crackling of thorns under a pot," must be released by the new song of St. Francis, the laughter of the Lord's foolhardy, who so compassionately loved every created thing and every man he met. The Christian is the only man who has any right to laugh, a pagan can only be jolly when he is drunk.

The gaiety of St. Francis was different in substance from other humorous laughter. It was not the eternal grin of the optimist, not the mirth of Mark Tapleys, not the tintinnabulation of the maid who

puts on laughter's lilt with a lipstick, not the guffaw
of the alcoholic escapist, and not the comic giggle of
the comedian. It belonged to none of these death-
doomed laughters. But when we ask what was the
secret of his laughter we are conscious of another
contradiction: for his song's ultimate theme was
suffering such as few saints have known. His song
was consummated not by Milton's "laughter holding
both her sides" but by the Stigmata of the crucified
Christ on his hands and feet.

The laughter of St. Francis was the laughter of a
great certainty. He knew his Savior with a certainty
that made all earthly phenomena shimmery, iridescent words of God made flesh. St. Francis laughed
because he was not worried about security. He knew
that God could drop the whole universe at any
moment if he so willed. But he knew that when God
forgave, he clasped the world once and for all. St.
Francis felt himself cupped by the pierced hands of
his Lord as a candle is cupped by the hands of a
housewife.

St. Francis laughed because he had no fear. He
was so certain of God's love that he never dreamed
there could be hate in the heart of a wolf or of a
Saracen soldier or a robber of the wild hills. Certainty about God made him carefree about man. His
exquisite and never-failing tact in dealing with all
sorts and conditions of men was inspired by the smile

in his eyes. St. Francis sang a roundelay because his heart was quiet at the center. He could jest like Sir Thomas More. There is no real fun without faith. There is no true song without certainty. It was a frequent exclamation of St. Teresa of Avila, "God deliver me from sullen saints."

The laughter of St. Francis was the laughter that follows renunciation. Impedimenta choke singing. The Happy Man is always he who has no symbolic shirt to his back. Bunyan's Pilgrim found, that the pack on his back choked his song: he broke into song when he lost his load. The smallest thing in the world is as heavy as sin itself when it is clung to against God's will. When St. Francis tore off his father's embroidered coat and tossed his money upon it, he put on the garment of joy for the spirit of heaviness. When he begged the crust that the dogs would not eat, he washed it down with the royal wine of joy. Faced with the renunciation entailed in celibacy (he who had once composed love songs for the gold and crimson pageantry of the joust), he perpetrated the excellent jest of making imaginary figures of wife and children with frozen hands out of the snow, muttering delightedly, "These must be clothed. See, poor things, they are dying of cold; here there will be all kinds of trouble." And by his renunciation he blessed a multitude of marriages, and by his love made ten thousand children laugh.

St. Francis laughed because he found that he possessed all since he owned nothing. Like St. Ignatius of Loyola he prayed, "Only give me thy love and thy grace, and I will count myself rich: and will ask for nothing more." Such laughter is immortal, singing beyond death, echoing when the world shall be dust and the bright stars are quenched.

He laughs longest who laughs last.

CHAPTER 4

Wedding Bells

I HAVE LIKENED the joy of the coming of St. Francis to the lyrical rapture of spring. This time I would penetrate deeper, lest readers should think that I reduce the happiness of the saint to the level of the sentimentalism of the lover of Nature. There is a positive note in Christian joy. It arises not merely from a sense of well-being—the tra-la-la of the spring troubadour—but from the supernatural joy of consecration. The joy in the heart of the Prodigal Son was different in quality from the good cheer of his elder brother when he gave a feast. The Prodigal Son was beaten to grateful knees by an amazing forgiveness and the bells of Heaven echoed in his heart, for he was a repenting sinner and not one of the ninety-nine who knew no repentance.

And so I might change the whole metaphor and speak of the joy of the Wedding Bells of St. Francis. Not so much of a metaphor either, for St. Francis did indeed engage in holy matrimony—he wedded my

Lady Poverty. That expresses the utter consecration to one he loved—so utterly did he love his chosen bride that no ordinary love-letter glows with such rapture of words. It is told that at the last frolic of his youth, his boon companions enthroned him as Lord of Misrule. There on that tinsel throne he sat, far away in thought. This silenced the revelers, who began to grin and whisper, "Look, he's in love!" St. Francis sensed their meaning. "Yes, I am in love," he said; "I am about to marry a lady fairer and purer than you could possibly imagine." This Lady Poverty, by the intensity of his thought became more and more objective and real. He saw her in all things and at last in a vision he beheld her with our Savior on the Cross. This was the antithesis of a "complex"—it was the wholly healthy and complete sublimation of earthly love. He was not a man beset, but a man set free.

Now, St. Francis was a child of the age of romance. The orgiastic Venus worship of paganism had been christened by the Church and had broken out in poetic chivalry. Young men chose a fair one and raised her on a throne of reverence, flaunted her name on their lances, affected fierce jealousy of her honor, broke out like singing birds into ballades. The Troubadour was the ballad monger of idealistic love. It was like the literalness of St. Francis that he should choose a bride who would demand real sacrifices, not mere roundelays of song—a broken will, not a shattered spear.

The element of supernatural grace was seen in the amazing fact that thousands of rich young men joined in the bridal ceremony and joyfully fell in love with poverty. Multitudes of the type of the rich young man who sorrowing turned his back on Jesus, did actually give all to the poor and embrace poverty.

And so I join issue with Abel Bonnard who, to my mind, fell a prey to the modern fallacies of the psychiatrists who from a study of perversion, attribute all psychological elements in a man's personality to the repressions (and repressed sins) of youth. There is a real danger that the psychiatrist may confuse the elemental reality of right and wrong, of moral responsibility, of the sense of guilt which prostrates the soul before the Cross. It was not to correct psychological kinks that Jesus Christ died on the Cross. He died to atone for the real and gigantic sin of mankind, to bring individual salvation to guilty souls—to such a degree that each soul feels that Christ died for him only.

> "Quaerens me, sedisti lassus,
> Redemisti, crucem passus,
> Tantus labor non sit cassus."

In all this I dispute with the good Abel Bonnard. He suggests that there was evidence in St. Francis of repressions created by the actual sinful passion of youth. If this were true, it would not affect the authenticity of the sainthood of St. Francis (witness the Confessions of St. Augustine). This is how Bonnard wrote: "He was all petulance, vivacity and charm. Indulgently brought up by his parents he found himself naturally as a youth at the head of the wealthy young men whose exploits were the talk of Assisi. Up to the age of twenty-five, Francis led the most dissipated life. He was the king of a band he was always leading to new follies. *It is difficult to say how far these extravagances went* (italics mine). It is certain, however, that he was always very prone to carnal desires. It was to mortify these that he rolled among thorns and in snow. Once when the people were praising him as a saint, he replied he was not yet out of danger, since he was still of an age to have a wife and children. That he should have specified this among all the temptations that assailed him, shows what he felt to be his weakness . . . Besides, in his profane youth, *Francis was always singing, and of what do songs speak but of love?*" (Italics mine.)

To me this is sheer nonsense, and not very nice-minded of the good Bonnard. There is a slight if unconscious leer in his phrase, "difficult to say how far" . . . This is the very language of those who gain vicarious pleasure from speculating on the details of the sins of others. That St. Francis should have re-

buked the flatterers by reminding them that he was
of marriageable age is no basis for Bonnard's Freudian
suggestion. It was more like a laughing joke. And
surely it is a gross misunderstanding of bodily morti-
fication to link it with only one weakness. But Bonnard let the cat out of the psychological bag when he
wrote quite deliciously, "of what do songs speak but
of love?" Truly the Troubadour's songs were all on
the theme of love, but love conventionalized, de-
vitalized, romanticized by the poetic sentimentalities
of the current chivalry. One might as well say that
because some Canadian soldier sang "Roll out the
barrel" he was agonizing to control his Bacchanalian
desires, whereas he might be an austere devotee of
soft drinks. Next we shall have a psychiatrist at-
tributing Dante's devotion to Beatrice to a youthful
complex. No, there is a hint of "snooping" in this
attitude and we shall be nearer the truth if we see
in young Francis a fiery youth full of romantic ideals
and absurd chivalries, quite eager to anticipate Love-
lace when he wrote:

>   "I could not love thee dear, so much,
>
>   Loved I not honor more."

Whatever of carnal desire there was in the young
Francis was transmuted by the all absorbing supernatural life in his soul. Christ was the first love of
Saint Clare; she could never have been the first love
of St. Francis.

Let us come out into the fresh air—in which St. Francis lived—out from the speculations of the Viennese laboratory. Read the songs of St. Francis. Of what do they sing? Not only of love, good Bonnard, but of Wind and Fire and Water and singing Bird, of Sun, of Trees. Never before had such songs broken the hush of dawn. They set children and birds and sinners singing too. They were the songs of a world redeemed. The prophecy of the Psalmist was fulfilled: "He hath put a new song into my mouth."

This is the song the world needs today. We brood upon our frustrations: we psycho-analyze our souls; we hanker after the things we have not and are not content with what we have. Fear and hatred stalk like spectres in the councils of men; ideologists argue feverishly about ownership of property, public and private. Oh for the song of St. Francis, the song that tells of all morbidities cleansed by the love and forgiveness of God, of childlike faith that Christ has our case in his pierced hands, that all we have and hold are God's, not ours, and must be flung at his feet! The song of St. Francis—of the man who, owning nothing, possessed all, and made the towns of Umbria ring with the wedding bells of my Lady Poverty!

Do you remember Masseo's reply to the enquirer? "He who has but one joy has but one song."

CHAPTER 5

The New Song of St. Francis

BUT I MUST go on stressing even at the risk of reiteration, the significance of the joy of St. Francis. We may lay too much stress on him as Le Jongleur de Dieu. It was a Savior's love, not a sanguine liver, that gave him to laughter. His joy was the highest a human soul may know; learned doctors have even speculated whether it is not higher than the joy of angels—the joy of the forgiven. The earth he trod was lit by the gleam of a pristine spring because it was an old world redeemed. Every man was beautiful and lovable, because the blessed Savior died for him. I knew a man, who, when he walked out into the street after making his first confession, saw the world "appareled in celestial light, the glory and the freshness of a dream."

In only one of the parables of Jesus, I think, does the story rise to lyric rapture. The Prodigal Son had come home (what shallow literateur wrote: "It is better to travel than to arrive"?). There is the whole

gamut of human emotion between David's cry,
"Absalom, my son!" and the cry of the father, "This
is my son, come home! Come home!" Oh, there were
rings on the Prodigal's fingers and around him
thrown the gleaming cloak of joy; there was feast-
ing and fun and song and dance. Jesus makes us
feel the palpitating jollity of it all. Why? Because a
satiated ragged sinner had repented and tramped
home with bleeding feet. And Jesus opened the
silent sky and let us hear the bells of Heaven jubilant-
ly ringing. Now that was the joy of St. Francis.

But I do not believe it was only a personal joy.
His mind was too objective for overmuch self-analysis.
Perhaps the main inspiration of his joy was joy
that the mankind he knew was emerging from the
Dark Ages of Dreadful Penance into the more lucid
day of a realized forgiveness.

During what we call the Dark Ages the Church
had to grapple with that diabolical corruption and
dreadful bias of sin which seeped down from the
Greek and Roman civilizations and the demons of
the pagan gods. The dawn-light of reason, which
had shone over the blue Aegean, grew dim as the
worship of beauty and the cult of the healthy body
turned to unmentionable and unnatural corruption
which tainted even the starry philosophers with its
lustful lunacy. As G. K. Chesterton wrote: "Pan
was nothing but panic, and Venus nothing but

venereal vice." If this was Byron's "glory that was Greece", what of his "grandeur that was Rome?" That grandeur broke and blossomed in Nero the sadist. The conflict of the Church with this corruption was dark, dreadful, shot through with strange cruelties, black hatred and fierce penance. But the disease was stayed in its center and source, leaving civilization scarred.

This was the great pessimism of God; the Divine pessimism of "when there was no eye to pity and no arm to save." Then, as G. K. Chesterton again wrote, came the good tidings of Original Sin. Good tidings? Good tidings? Yes, for the corollary of Original Sin is Supernatural Grace. "When there was no eye to pity and no arm to save, *then* his own eye pitied and his own arm saved."

Perhaps this is overmuch to simplify and to dramatize, but we may view the world of St. Francis as staggering out of that nightmare and blinking in the silver dawn of a springtime come again. Men were sullen, rubbed eyes and knew not what to do. Then came the sounding of a hearty laugh: the tide of the joy of a world redeemed was forced through the heart of St. Francis, and he laughed. Then many men laughed. What Chaucer did for English poetry, St. Francis did for the Christian religion—he made it sing and glisten with dew.

So runs my dream. For I do not apprehend that

his joy sprang from mere temperament. It was not the hilarious ha-ha of the man who was happy because he had not a shirt to his back, but the joy of the infinitely rich; he tied a sack around him, but it was the festive robe of forgiveness; his was not the new wine of perfect juvenility of health; he had drunk of The Spirit. He did not fool and sing because he had left behind the irksome control of his home; his was the joy of the son who had come home.

Only, the home was very big. So big that even he thought the far-off Sultan might be a brother in it. Certainly the larks nested in its garth and all flowers grew in its perennial borders.

This then is the joy supreme on earth and in Heaven. It is the new song put into the mouth of men. The forgiven soul pours forth gratitude in every thought, word and deed of life, and death is only the sunset time when singing birds fold their wings and break to song anew in the everlasting Dawn.

May our blessed Lord give us the joy of St. Francis.

CHAPTER 6

St. Francis As Poet

IT IS THE PLAY of those who denigrate the Church
to deplore the sinners of the Catholic Church and to
ignore the saints; which is to criticize the discontented garden's winter and to be blind to the dogmatic crocus which calls with golden bugle, "Spring
is here." They see stony deserts but not the heavenly
bread let us say of Thomas a Kempis in his *Imitatio
Christi*. At Christmastide they smile at the "legend"
of the gift-bearing Wise Men, but forget the historic
fact that a royal band of artists brought their gifts
of gold and frankincense and myrrh to the Madonna
and the Child—Fra Angelico, Fra Filippo Lippi,
Piero della Francesca, Sandro Botticelli, Domenico
del Ghirlandajo, Leonardo da Vinci, Pietro Perugino,
and Raphael. They leap from Virgil to John Milton,
and omit Dante the poet of the Middle Ages. Martin
Luther and Raphael were born in the same year,
and for every one who reads the sermons of Luther,
ten thousand learn God's courtesy before the

Madonnas of Raphael. Ghirlandajo died when Luther was a boy of eleven, and for every one who reads Luther's denunciations of the rebellious peasants ten thousand learn God's loving-kindness before Ghirlandajo's "Adoration of the Shepherds."
Of the critics we may say:

"Only they see not God, I know,
Nor all that chivalry of his,
The soldier-saints who, row on row,
Burn upward each to his point of bliss."

Now there was a time when fewer buds and blossoms were seen in the landscape of the Church. But suddenly there sounded the springsong of a bird divine—the song of St. Francis of Assisi.

St. Francis was a poet. Nobody can understand St. Francis unless he sees that fact. Not the author of a poetic legend—a poet himself! The revelations of a poet are intensely individual. His mind is a prism on which the white light of God breaks in iridescent colors. The words of a poet are "semantic"—they fructify in the soul's mystic deeps; their music soars above their meaning, vibrates in the inward ear of the mind, and the listener hears "a silver trumpet blown from the hid battlements of eternity."
"Sounds of vernal showers,
On the twinkling grass,
All that ever was
Joyous and clear and fresh, thy music doth surpass."

St. Francis was neither St. Thomas Aquinas, the
angelic doctor, nor St. Augustine, the angelic philosopher. He was the mystic of the metaphor, the saint
of the simile—the poet. To him the eternal Word
was set to music; there was rhyme and reason in
all things, but he was more sensitive to the rhyme.

St. Francis, moreover, was a lyric poet. He would
have loved Keats's *Ode to a Nightingale,* and might
have been bored by Milton's *Paradise Lost.* He did
not view history as a heroic epic poem unfolding
canto by canto, book by book, to the vast epilogue
of the Dies Irae. The world to him was a garden
full of inspirations for lyric songs. Rivers ran brightly
through glittering vales, paradisal meadows were
fragrant with blossoms, the dew sparkled in orient
light on grass of God's own green. He had no abstract ideas about Nature—nothing of Wordsworth's
philosophic abstractions. To him every offspring of
Nature was an individual being, bright and breathing. Brothers Wind and Water and Fire he knew
and praised; birds were little sisters, the bad wolf
was a misunderstood sinner who craved for a hand-
shake. He even made a lyric out of frozen feet. He
dramatized, personalized, everybody and everything.
While the roystering companions of his youth were
laughing in purposeless alliance with the day's pin-up
girls of Assisi, he was ravished with the beauty of my

Lady Poverty and desired to be wed to her.

Perhaps we may say that the influence which St. Francis wielded over men and women is the breath of a lyric poet. We may not understand his words, but we hear a music of divine sweetness; we are enchanted before we are converted. His converts repented by becoming young again; their penance was to do the foolish heroic things poets do; they deserted the plough and the potter's wheel and followed the Pied Piper of Assisi. That is why the over-maligned Friar Elias was called in at last. He was merely an efficient bureaucrat. An official document had to be compiled from a lyric, and rapture had to be mobilized—which indeed is the appropriate work of the bureaucrat in every age.

But the lyric of St. Francis is immortal and sounds wherever there are harpstrings quivering in the longing heart. The weary and the dreary still lift their hearts to listen to the exquisite music of a dream. The lyric of St. Francis is a bar of that melody that ravished creation when the morning stars sang together, a part of the carol which the angels sang to the shepherds in Bethlehem's fields. We shall not hear its like again until we recognize it, piercing sweet, in the angel chorus singing out of the ever-folding Rose about God's throne.

"The high that proved too high, the heroic for
    earth too hard,
  The passion that left the ground, to lose itself
    in the sky,
Are music sent up to God, by the lover and the
    bard,
  Enough that he heard it once—we shall hear
    it by and by."

CHAPTER 7

St. Francis As Dramatist

Now I THINK of St. Francis as a dramatist. How naturally my friend Father Declan has found that the episodes of his life may be made into one-act plays. His story is not a tome of philosophy, not an epic poem, not an essay, not a novel with its pyschological analysis; it is drama. From the very beginning every step of his way was felt as a dramatic act, a play. There was always the stage and the *mise en scene;* the actors, the swift play of dialogue, the decisive action and the emphatic curtain. The only time he was baffled was when the skilled administrators came to him with a scheme of organization. He could not see the order under the new rules as a drama. It would not act for him. He could not simplify a constitution; and the genius of the dramatist works by intense simplification.

St. Francis called everybody into his acting company, and every living thing. Angels, lepers, merchants, bishops, robbers. Of course these—but also the wolf, the dove, the birds, the sun and wind and trees and flowers and running water. He would not have them static or purposeless. They must act.

He gave meaning to the fierce old wolf. Being a dramatist, he made the wolf act something; made him shake hands. If it were possible, I would make a gift to children: a toy theatre set of the plays of St. Francis. What a company, what thrilling scenes! And if Father Declan's plays could be acted by the children of all our churches—what a gospel!

St. Francis the dramatist: every scene of his life stands out lucid and dramatic, cut down to the uttermost simplicity. That throwing of his rich coat at his father's feet and marching out into the world in sackcloth; how could St. Francis help but make a complete scene of it? That subduing of the robber band—the drama of Robin Hood has had to borrow from it! Shakespeare's Mark Antony speech does not rival the effect produced by St. Francis wherever he appeared! "Bells rang, the merchant left his desk, the trader his counter, the workman his tools", and the children cried "Ecco il santo." Men touched the hem of his tunic and women kissed his footprints on the ground. "Friends, Romans, Countrymen," sounds tame after this.

Think of the drama of the young and beautiful Lady Clare. It is the classic drama of St. Francis. I marvel that a play has never been done around this story, rivaling G. B. Shaw's St. Joan. All the elements of a great drama are there. The beautiful patrician girl, stirred by strange dreams and deep discontents; eager talk with her sister Agnes about the saint who was teaching Umbria a new song and calling to a new way of life; messages to and from St. Francis; the tryst at the Porziuncula; a night with a wild moon riding; Clare creeping through the doors of her castle home, climbing the walls, escaping from proud, severe aristocratic parents and brothers; the guiding torches in the woods; the hands of St. Francis raised to bless her. "Falling prostrate before the altar of the Virgin in silent prayer, she took the vows of poverty, chastity and obedience. Her rich and noble robes she exchanged for coarse sackcloth, her jeweled girdle for a cincture of rope, her lovely golden tresses, shorn by Francis's own hand, fell at her feet which were no longer adorned with silken hose but thrust naked into rough wooden sandals."

Father Declan had no difficulty in composing a moving drama of the deathbed of St. Francis; his joyous singing of the praise of Brother Death from his Canticle of Brother Sun; the inspired visit of his friend the Lady Jacqueline (even the humorous interlude of Brother Juniper, the cook); the cry of the mourners, "Father, Father, what shall we do?"; the laying of the body on the naked earth, the singing of the birds—a great and moving drama. As Milton wrote in *Samson Agonistes:*

"Nothing is here for tears, nothing to wail
Or knock the breast; no weakness, no contempt,
Dispraise or blame; nothing but well and fair,
And what may quiet us in a death so noble."

St. Francis was a dramatist because he possessed tremendous vitality. This vitality functioned as a radiance flaming from an inner source, and like the blacksmith's bellows at the forge, keeping his imagination at white heat. Yet this was not merely the physiological vitality of those men who are "bulls in a china shop." With St. Francis it was a pure flame of life. The creative glow which passed from him, imparted life to those persons and things which are puppets only to the earthbound poet and essayist and novelist. His plays were not puppet-shows with actors manipulated by wires controlled by his nimble fingers. When St. Francis passed by they came to life like the sleeping beauty of Tennyson's poem:

"A touch, a kiss! The charm was snapt!
There rose a noise of striking clocks,
And feet that ran, and doors that clapt,
And barking dogs, and crowing cocks;

A fuller light illumined all,
A breeze thro' all the garden swept,

And sudden hubbub shook the hall,
    And sixty feet the fountain leapt,"
Yes, that was it—
   "And all the long-pent stream of life
    Dashed downward in a cataract."

That is why he was a dramatist. At his touch all and everything became aware and significant figures in a drama of which he was the star. Boys make a snowman, but it does nothing but look odd and anon it melts. But the snowman which the saint made, played opposite St. Francis. Together they acted an interlude in the manner of Shakespeare's clowns. Here is how Msgr. Ronald Knox tells it:

"When he felt tempted, one extremely cold night, to regret his vows, he got up out of bed, and went out into the snow just as he was, and made a snow woman and six snow children; and he pretended that they were his wife and family. 'There,' he said to himself—for he talked to himself as all children do—'these must be clothed; see, poor things, they are dying of cold; here there will be all kinds of trouble.' "

In a flash of insight he adds that the Poor Man of Assisi and the Little Flower of Lisieux stretch out hands to one another across the centuries, as if they were two children playing a game.

A mighty work was accomplished by St. Thomas Aquinas, whose mind ranged through the universe of things and brought all into the harmony of God. Here are his volumes, a monument to all times. St. Francis could do nothing of this. But drawing aside the curtain of the material and turning on the footlights of no earthly radiance, he gave us the sharp swift clash of comedy and tragedy, so that abstractions strutted as living actors on the stage.

And some have seen mankind's story as a tremendous drama. Salvation came not as a thesis, but as a message by an angel to the Ancilla Domini chosen before time was, as the Babe born in the manger heralded by a star and an angelic choir, with simple shepherds and wise kings as chorus. And at the last against the blackest cloud of judgment known to the world, the Cross was "placarded" (as St. Paul himself said) as the flaming sign and symbol and assurance to men. A Protestant hymn writer grasped the truth when he wrote *"Tis done! 'Tis done! The great transaction's done."*

CHAPTER 8

The Charming Saint

IN THIS CHAPTER I wish to gather up and under-line the truths discussed in the preceding pages.

I read once of a charming talk given by a radio padre on St. Francis. The padre of course, was more than charming. But in my professional and social life I have come to suspect and dread "charming" men. So invariably their charm is the magnetic effulgence of selfishness—the weapon deliberately used to exploit others. Their charming personality is an easy substitute for moral rectitude and the con-secrated will. Don Juan and King Charles the Sec-ond were charming men. Women, perhaps, are prone to prefer charm to strength.

The truth is (and first I admonish myself) that we Franciscans must de-sentimentalize St. Francis, rescue him from the spring poets and sloppy poseurs, the hearty humanists, and the host of the hail-fellow-well-met. We must bring out the fact that the virtue of St. Francis springs from supernatural grace and cultivation, and not from natural charm. We must see pictures of him other than the poet picking flowers, or trilling to the trees, or having fun with skylarks, or wagging paws with a wolf. We must see him with bleeding hands laying stone on stone at a ruined church; with frozen feet in the snows of Umbria; with hungry teeth munching mouldy bread; in poignant prayer and fierce fasting; in the Gethsemane which set the stigmata on him; in the agony of frustrated ideals; in the blindness and pain of a dying body; in his merciless rebukes and dire denunciation of sin. The nobleman and the ploughman who first shared his begged bread, learned to respect him before they loved him. This applies to all Christians. Men must learn to respect us before they love us. And it is true of husbands; and wives also.

But there! In an age when men elect God as a member of their club and make the Lord Christ a crony in their crusade for a kindly communism, it is no wonder that the piercing look in the eyes of St. Francis, as he visualizes sin, should be belied by his charming smile; and that the picturesque cloak and the bunch of flowers should be emphasized at the cost of the frozen feet and blinded eyes. Men will share his songs who will not make his sacrifice; and will chant his roundelays who will not cry for mercy at the foot of the Cross.

Moreover, St. Francis has been roped into the youth movement of today. The idea which largely animates this movement, is that youth shall be attracted and given gifts of entertainment, whereas it is obvious that their need is that discipline and loyalty which subdue natural passions. The Boy Scout is offered hardship and adventure, and loves it. But "youth" (that unfortunate abstraction) is offered a jolly club, a room warm and bright, and dance floors. A shallow reading of a paragraph in a book of Sabatier's did something to foster this fallacy. It pictures the Franciscan century as a youth of twenty with an old-fashioned Church too decrepit to attract youth. The truth was, as Sabatier admitted, that the Church was too troubled with hardened old heretics to be bothered about youth. The Pope gave his blessing to St. Francis because he rejoiced in his youth, and Sabatier went on to say that this blessing given to St. Francis proved that the Church itself possessed perennial youth. But the youth sacrificed ease and wealth, and was willing to be frozen and starved! The Pope did not set up a youth club in Rome; he sent St. Francis on the crusade of the ruthless cross! The Pope knew the heart of the young man better than the psychiatrist of today. I have read the story of St. Francis carefully, and cannot find that boys and girls, or grown folks either, neglected home to flock after him. St.

Francis, who founded the Third Order, was too wise to tempt boys and girls away from home and parental control. The true fourth movement is the movement back to the home, not to nights out with all the fun of the fair.

Then, we may deride sentimental talk about the "ordinary man." To certain sociologists, mankind is divided into two classes: the intellectuals, professionals, pyschiatrists, dramatists, aristocrats; and the rest, consisting of that amazing person the Ordinary Man. Thus an honored friend said that the secret of St. Francis lay in this human kinship with ordinary folks, backed with an equally natural kinship to God. I find these phrases misleading. What man confesses himself "ordinary"? Is he not aware of his intense and lonely individuality, and his repentance? Does he go as a member of a deputation to the Savior, or as the only person in the world whom Christ died to save? "Quaerens *me,* sedisti lassus—Seeking *me* thou didst drop down weary."

And what does "natural kinship to God" mean? Is not that broken by the deep damnation of original sin? Are we not saved by supernatural grace, or saved not at all? Grace is not natural; it is of God. It is the increate love of the Godhead. And so the fact is that St. Francis was utterly unaware of ordinary men or extraordinary men. He saw no difference, except in their piety, between noblemen and

peasants and lawyers and robbers. Every man to him
was the Only Man in the World, and a man waiting
to be saved. If he became the friend of the poor,
he was not a class devotee. There just happened to
be more poor than rich in the world, and he was a
poor man too. St. Francis knew nothing of a bread-
and-circus proletariat. Each single man was marvelously made and still more marvelously redeemed.
We shall not be judged in batches at the last day.
We shall stand solitary and alone before the all-
seeing and pitying eyes of our Father God.

The Charming Saint? No, and never!

"There goes a very dangerous man."

"Dangerous to whom, Holy Father?" interrupted
Cardinal Ugolino. "To the Devil", smiled the great
wise Pope, "dangerous to the Devil, my son."

CHAPTER 9

Gethsemane

THE STIGMATA OF FRANCIS, the impressing of the wounds of the crucified Christ does not belong to the realm of legend. It is a firmly authenticated fact of history.

First of all, the experience was unique in the annals of the Christian faith. There was nothing to predispose the Franciscan friars to expect so astounding a phenomenon. It was so new a manifestation that it made a sharp and pristine impression on their minds. It is evident from the records that the brethren of St. Francis were in a state of wonder and awe as they witnessed a passion of prayer so intense and prolonged and supernatural that it was beyond their comprehension. They must have anticipated some kind of Divine consummation, some apocalypse may be, some miracle in the death of their saint, but they could not have dreamed that the result of his ecstasy would be the imprinting the

44

wounds of the Cross on the body of their master. The stigmata of St. Francis were unique.

But St. Francis did not come to his friars and show them the stigmata; he hid them away. The presence and reality of them the friars had to discover as they journeyed with him and tended his person. They were filled with wonder, but their eyes beheld and they had to believe. Their testimony is embodied in *I Fioretti di S. Francesco* (The Little Flowers of St. Francis), which is a free translation of a Latin original based on the records, written and oral, of the saint's most intimate disciples. They lived long to discourse of the stigmata. St. Clare survived St. Francis by twenty-seven years, Friar Giles by thirty-five, and Friar Leo, the beloved secretary, who swathed his master's wounds, lived longer than they. Sabatier made a discovery in Assisi which proves that the Lady Giacoma, the noble friend whom St. Francis summoned from Rome to his deathbed and who revered his wounds, was still living in 1273—so that the living testimony continued for some fifty years after the death of St. Francis. Cardinals investigated and were convinced. Pope Gregory believed. Thousands of peasants who hailed St. Francis on his way to his final home saw evidence of the stigmata in his bandaged hands. And so the reality of the stigmata was affirmed by those who should best know. It is not a legend, it is a fact.

Another curious kind of evidence is provided by those who explain the stigmata as the morbid marks of an abnormal psychological state. They therefore accept the fact of the stigmata, but deny their Divine origin. Now it is accepted that intense emotion may permanently affect the body. And nobody will question the fact that never was there a more intense emotion than the self-identification of Francis with the crucified Christ. At the same time to believe that the strongest human emotion is capable of producing permanent new body tissue, such as were the nail-form excrescences on the body of St. Francis, is to ascribe to mere human emotion a creative power, an interference with natural processes, which your same miracle-shy objector does not concede to the almighty Maker himself. Much simpler to take the stigmata as the orthodox take them: as an external, physical miracle of nature as well as an internal marvel of grace!

It would be illuminating if we followed a brief outline of the stages by which St. Francis reached this unique consummation in Christ. And to understand that, it is necessary to look back and see what had happened to the vast order which St. Francis had founded. This at once leads to a comment on a general principle which operates in all movements begun in pure enthusiasm and succeeding beyond expectation.

Fully to explicate this we should read the noble volume written by Msgr. Ronald Knox, the harvest of a lifetime of study on the subject of the "enthusiasms" which have shaken men and provoked reaction by the Church in every age. Our Lord appears to be the only one who estimated aright the nature of such enthusiasm and made provision for its preservation through organization and discipline. He trained men to be the apostles of a Church. The Church was to harness enthusiasm. Faith without enthusiasm grows stale and unprofitable. Yes, enthusiasm without disciplined faith can run to dangerous excesses and degenerate into lawless zeal.

When St. Francis threw aside his patrician coat and donned sackcloth, he launched a movement of the purest enthusiasm known in the history of evangelism. The Pope blessed him. Francis went forward with single-minded devotion to the Church. His original theme was poverty—a poverty so real to him that he romantically wed himself to her. It spelt the utter giving up of all a man had or held, not in property only but in everything that savored of self. Like the birds his friars were to become pensioners of God. He based himself on verse three of the ninth chapter of St. Luke's Gospel: "Take nothing with you to use on your journey, staff or wallet or bread or money; you are not to have more than one coat apiece." Perhaps also the closing

passages of the chapter were in mind: "The man
said to him, I will follow thee wherever thou art
going. But Jesus told him, Foxes have holes, and
the birds of the air their nesting places, the Son
of Man has nowhere to lay his head. To another
he said, Follow me, and he answered, Lord, give me
leave to go home and bury my father first. But
Jesus said to him, Leave the dead to bury their
dead." (Ronald Knox translation.)

The astonishing fact is that a multitude of all
sorts and conditions of men were obedient to the
ideal; they begged crusts; they endured cruel priva-
tions in exposure and cold, and still the enthusiasm
mounted as the joyous Francis sang his way through
Italy. All the world, so it seemed to his disciples,
went after him. So much so that Francis himself
recognized that if all followed him the mills would
fall to ruin and the fields rot and homes decay. As
we shall see when we study the Third Order in Part
III, he himself commanded people to stay at home
and to hold all in trust for God in penitence and
service. He had to explain to his Friars that poverty
was not mendicancy and that it was better for the
Friars to learn an honorable handicraft and to beg
food only in emergencies.

In plain fact, Francis's mighty creation grew beyond the control of its founder. St. Francis is the
supreme saint of the passion of evangelism, but the

enthusiast is rarely a statesman. St. Francis was not
the man capable of transforming his order into an
integral part of the Holy Catholic Church. He became aware that parasites were creeping in; he
pilloried "Friar Fly, who plied his jaws more than
his hands." He began to realize that the public was
having its misgivings; he took recourse to the Church,
seeking a Cardinal Protector who under the authority
of the Pope would defend the order against its
"detractors."

Then, too, being the man he was—an utter in-
dividualist intent on the way before him—St. Francis
was not touched by certain wider movements which
were stirring the minds of men in those times of
ferment. The passion for beauty and knowledge
which marked the early thirteenth century influenced
many Franciscans. They felt that intellectual and
artistic needs as well as purely religious needs were
a demand of the day on them for the good of God's
cause. They desired somehow to integrate the Franciscan ideal and the demands which a living, stirring world was making on their imagination. Moreover, enthusiasm was playing its part in disintegrat-
ing the orderly Church life of the provinces. Ministers of churches complained of "vagrant imposters
trading on the reputation of the order."

By all this St. Francis was bewildered and for him
brightness fell from the air. On May 21, 1221, a

great chapter general was held, attended by nearly 5000 friars. The chapter formulated certain new regulations. A demand for closer discipline made itself felt and with it the demand for living conditions making such discipline possible. On this point it was, if not on this occasion, that for the first, *and last,* time Francis came nigh to bitter denunciation. He did not realize he was treading the pathway of all the great enthusiasts and saviors of the world. As time went on, he was forced to the admission, that, human nature being what it is, his ideal was not workable except among a select comparative few. This admission was presently followed by the realization that he was no longer the man to govern the order. He abdicated as minister general in 1221. Though apparently a measure of discretionary authority remained his to the end, he began more and more to follow his bent toward the retired life of contemplation, content to do his bit with prayer and good example rather than by active participation in the affairs of the order.

It would, however, be wrong to conclude that "almost everything that was done in the order after 1221 was done without his knowledge or against his will." If nothing else, it was Francis who wrote and then re-wrote the final rule of the Friars approved in solemn form at Rome November 29, 1223, and Francis was in Rome for that occasion. He

came from Rome fortified with special authority
from the Pope to celebrate his special Christmas
Crib at Greccio—not the gesture of a broken man
but of a man happy in God, and happy in God to
the last; also, significantly, happiest of all in God
after La Verna. More careful recent research puts
almost all of his so-called writings in the years from
1221 to 1226, and striking in them (the later, the
more so) is his insistence on obedience, in support
of the major problem confronting the order in these
years.

At no time was there a sullen, sulking, rebellious
Francis—that, even under the circumstances, would
have ranked him beneath so gloriously many tried
souls. It would most certainly not have put him,
a flaming seraph of Divine love, at their head. It
would not have placed him by the side of his Master,
who "set his face to go toward Jerusalem," not in
a mood of defeatism, not in resentment toward those
who were proffering him the cup of sorrow, not
in self-pity—to think that he had failed!—but in
resolute obedience to his Father's will. The Cross
in the case of our Lord was not the defeat of a
prophet—it was the victory of the Savior—of Him
who for love of God defeated and conquered everything that otherwise conquers man and makes him
the slave of Sin.

In that spirit Francis entered on his Gethsemane,

his *via crucis*. God's will, pointed out to him in God's dispensation and the guidance of Mother Church, meant more to him than cherished ideals, more than personal humiliation, more than heart-ache over ties of companionship disappointed. Here was Lady Poverty, despoiled not only of things material, but of inmost self!

The treading of his *via crucis* itself—that con-centration of earthly suffering and supernatural de-light—was a long and complicated story. I can write of things only as they flash on my mind.

St. Francis paid "under obedience" that last visit to Rome, where he was received with honor and courtesy by the cardinals. But his soul was in prison amid what to him was luxury; he yearned for his beloved countryside and the companionship of Lady Poverty. Yet in that forlornness his quaint tender-ness never left him. Lady Giacoma comforted him. He brought her in return a little lamb. "It will make you think," he said, "of the Lamb of God, and also of Brother Francis his own little disciple." So gentle was he in heartbreak. The homeward journey took him to the vale of Řieti. Christmas was nigh. "Oh, that it were possible to adore with the shepherds and the Magi of old!" The poet and the dramatist flamed in him and he set all his friends joyfully to make the first Crib of its kind in the history of the

Christian Faith. That Crib was as unique as the Stigmata.

The Crib has been poeticized, making the Nativity a lovely picture separated from the whole truth of the Incarnation of which the Cross is an integral part. To St. Francis the Crib meant more than a lovely legend; it was the beginning for him of an agonizing passion of prayer which mounted in intensity from that Christmas day until it was consummated by the Stigmata on the feast of the Elevation of the Cross. "Be thou found in me," he began to pray. He besought God that he might take up his cross anew.

When St. Francis was forty-three years of age, in the year 1224, he was inspired by God to set forth from the vale of Spoleto and journey into Romagna. There a rich and potent nobleman, Roland of Chiusi di Casentino, before attending some dinner celebration, came to St. Francis to discuss the salvation of his soul. St. Francis bade him go back and dine with his friends, and then return to talk about his soul. Roland, probably astonished at this urbanity, did so. When he came back, he offered to the saint a mountain in Tuscany called "La Verna, most proper for devout contemplation"; he sent fifty men of arms with the Friars to see if it were indeed worthy of St. Francis.

La Verna is an enchanting spot. The peak stands

out from a belt of hills around the paradisal scenery
of Casentino, which is drained by the upper waters
of the Arno. St. Francis gazed at the view with
rapture. The primeval forest called to his soul. Wild
creatures roamed fearless of man. Singing birds
flocked to him and alighted on his shoulders, prov-
ing to St. Francis that it was pleasing to God for
him to dwell there. Orlando himself came and helped
build a hut of boughs at the foot of a majestic beech
tree. "From that time," record the *Little Flowers,*
"he gave himself to unceasing prayer." It was about
this time that the Friars borrowed an ass from a
rude peasant to bear their sick master upwards. The
peasant's words, which appear on the title page of
this book, were: "So you are the man everybody
is fussing about? You had better see that you make
good, or you are going to have something to answer
for." St. Francis painfully descended from the ass
(how honored donkeys are in Christian story!) and,
kneeling before the peasant kissed his feet. The
peasant then believed that he was a saint: and this
was the divine humility of a saint conscious that he
was a sinner.

St. Francis went on "to make good." In vigils,
fastings, mortifications, and agonizing tribulation of
soul. He began to leave the earth and mount up on
the wings of prayer to meet his crucified Lord.

Three of his seven companions were Friar Masseo,

the wise and eloquent; Friar Angelo, a noble gentle-
man who had been a knight; and Friar Leo, beloved
of St. Francis because he was a man of pure simplicity. From the records they left behind we feel the
emotion of awed and bewildered minds. La Verna
was astir with whisperings and portents that shook
the material veil. The supernatural made Mount
La Verna tremble. Pathetically they note that a
falcon stationed itself by the saint's hut and beat
his wings to awaken the exhausted Francis to re-
newed passionate prayer. There were dark demonic
presences abroad also, tempting them, leering at their
master. There were strange voices, strange gleams
among the trees, strange fires in the heavens. They
stood by as helpless as the disciples in Gethsemane.
St. Francis was far, far away from them. Although
in his moments of earthly consciousness he spoke
gently to them, he wanted to be alone, to be remote
even from his beloved friends, to be alone face to
face with his Lord and Savior and his Lord's Cross.
Vigil followed vigil, with body tortured by the soul's
excess, with prayer mounting beyond mortal reach,
crisis after crisis until the consummation was achieved.
The resultant Stigmata were evidence that here was
penitence and prayer and rapturous love beyond
human telling.

I marvel at the inspired passage in the *Little
Flowers:* "Anon an angel appeared to them with

exceeding great splendor, who held a viol in his left
hand and a bow in his right; and as St. Francis
stood all dazed at the vision, the angel drew his bow
upwards across the viol, and straightway St. Francis
heard such sweet melody that it ravished his soul
and lifted him beyond all bodily sense, so that . . . he
doubted lest his soul had wholly parted from his
body, by reason of the unbearable sweetness, *if the
angel had drawn the bow downwards again.*" (The
italics are mine.)

Could any modern psychologist compose a more
sensitive interpretation of the mystic passion of St.
Francis? "If the angel had drawn the bow downwards again." For had the angel drawn the bow
downwards and completed the melody, St. Francis
had died there and then on the sweetness of an
intolerable pain.

Friar Leo, "the simplest of men of all the friars
and for that reason most beloved by Francis," is the
source of our knowledge of the consummating experience.

It was the month of September. St. Francis had
kept the feast of the Assumption, and the day of
the Exaltation of the Holy Cross had come. All the
currents of the being of St. Francis were set towards
the Cross. Before the break of day he prayed:

"O my Lord Jesus Christ, two graces do I pray
you to grant me before I die: the first, that while

I live I may feel in my body and in my soul, so far
as is possible, that sorrow, sweet Lord, which you
suffered in the hour of your bitterest passion; the
second is, that I may feel in my heart so far as may
be possible, the exceeding love, wherewith, O Son
of God, you were enkindled to endure willingly for
us sinners agony so great." Sublime arrogance of
the humblest of all the saints! This sublime and unconscious audacity is reflected in the story as set down
in the *Little Flowers:*

"St. Francis began to contemplate most devoutly
the suffering of Christ and his infinite love; and the
fervor of devotion waxed so within him that through
love and through compassion, *he was wholly changed
into Jesus. . . .*

"A seraph with six resplendent and flaming wings
with swift flight drew nigh to St. Francis and he
knew clearly that he had the form of a man crucified. . . . Joy had he, exceeding great, at the gracious
aspect of Christ, but on the other hand, seeing him
nailed to the cross, he suffered unspeakable grief and
compassion. . . . It was revealed by the Seraph that
the vision should be shown to him in order that he
might understand he was to be changed into the
express likeness of the crucified Christ, not by bodily
martyrdom but by spiritual fire. . . .

"Then the whole mount of La Verna seemed to
flame forth with dazzling splendor that illumined

all the mountains and valleys round about, as if it were the sun shining on the earth. Wherefore when the shepherds that were watching in the country saw the mountain aflame, they were sore afraid. . . .

"Do you know," said Christ, "what I have done to you? I have given you the stigmas which are the marks of my passion. . . ."

From this time on the twilight of blindness began to fall on the eyes of St. Francis. In a hut of reeds prepared by Clare near St. Damian's he composed the first parts of the *Canticle of Brother Sun*. A year after the vision on Mount La Verna he was in Rieti, called thither by Cardinal Ugolino, who had secured the services of an eminent oculist. This man slowly drew a red hot iron (which was gently admonished by St. Francis) across his face from ear to eyebrow. "It did no good," wrote Thomas of Celano curtly. Advised that his release was near at hand, Francis joyfully added the praise of Brother Death to the Canticle of Brother Sun. On the road to his beloved Porziuncola he stayed the litter bearers and lifted his hands in blessing on Assisi, the city of his birth. He received the Sacrament, appealed to the friars to cleave to holy Poverty, and sang the 142nd Psalm— *Voce mea ad Dominum clamavi.* "Thus," writes Thomas of Celano, "he welcomed death with a song —*mortem suscepit cantando.*" He asked to be divested of his habit and to be laid beneath the sky on the bare ground. A late lark was singing.

"Abide with me, fast falls the eventide" . . .

It was the fourth of October, 1226. The friars bowed their heads in the vast silence of death. The silence was broken by "the clangor of trumpets, the tolling of bells, the chanting of litanies," as the funeral cortege wound up the hill to Assisi. The Lady Clare and her sisters took a last look at the face of their father in Christ. They cried, "Father, Father, what shall we do?" St. Francis was soon to show them, for he began to live again in minds made better by his presence.

Part II

The Friends of St. Francis

CHAPTER 1

Brother Juniper — the Fool

WHEN IN THE BOOK OF REVELATION the promise was made, "Behold, I make all things new," no change in the substance of things was meant, but a change in the eye of the beholder. Original sin blinded the eyes of mankind. Adam saw the Garden (to use Wordsworth's lines) "appareled in celestial light, the glory and the freshness of a dream." But with Sin "shades of the prison house" closed down on a man's sight. Those who would reduce St. Francis to a poetic legend, speak as if he imagined that the world sparkled with newborn light lit by birds with strange sweet song and gracious animals and living whispering trees. But St. Francis by the grace of Christ saw reality and not a poetic illusion. We shall see green grass as it really is in the fields of Paradise! And on the day of judgment the judgment will be in the *seeing*—the seeing of ourselves as God sees us. In the words of Dies Irae

"Ingemisco tamquam reus,
Culpa rubet vultus meus."

Now when St. Francis looked at men and women, he saw the reality of them, that is to say, their actual character and their potential virtue in a unity of personality. It is indeed annoying how utterly oblivious he was to those distinctions of class and culture which weigh with any one of us, except he be under five years of age—or a dog! We may boast we are broadminded, that we disdain to take notice of meretricious adjuncts such as wealth, social status, intellectual distinction, the form and features of a man, his dress—and his accent! But subconsciously we register these things and they change our tone and influence our judgment. It is virtually impossible to be free from this bias. But I have searched the records of St. Francis and have found not a jot or tittle of evidence that he thought of these adjuncts; his eye went straight to the inner core of a man. He rejoiced all the more in the individuality of his friends because he saw in them all the basic reality. Whether a robber, a nobleman, a bishop, an intellectual, a Lady Clare, or a Lady Giacoma—or even the Soldan of Babylon—stood before him, he saw an immortal soul. Only when we are sure of the basic reality of a man, can we begin to be tactful—or even charitable. When Jesus was rebuked for permitting the prostrate woman to pour fragrance over his feet, he asked: "Simon, *seeest* thou this woman?" There is a searching emphasis on *"seeest."* Simon did not see deep enough; he saw a trampled rose; Jesus saw a lily of God struggling up from the mud.

Now St. Francis was gifted with this in-sight of his Master. He had learned that from Jesus. His story carefully relates how he, like a good shepherd, knew all the merits and virtues of his companions and likewise their fastings. I intentionally omitted the operative phrase. The text adds "by divine revelation." Even so it was a second-hand in-sight; Jesus saw first.

The relationship of St. Francis with the poor fool, Brother Juniper, the figure of fun in the Franciscan story, reveals that he was oblivious of those distinctions of culture which count for so much with the intellectual. He suffered a fool gladly, not because fools amused him (that is a subtle form of snobbery), but because he recognized that fools were those who were marked by a simplicity carried out with swift and laughable logic. Take Brother Juniper, then, as an example. The virtue of both Brother Francis and Brother Juniper lay in their literalness. They were both literalists, except that Brother Francis took God literally while Brother Juniper took everything literally. That is the authentic Catholic note. Renan and the Humanists did not take Christ literally, they saw him through a pink mist of poetry.

St. Francis took things—and God—literally. Poverty to him was not a pose or a psalm about being poor—it was to possess nothing. If he talked about building a church, it was not to form a committee or to raise a fund. It meant carrying stones and mortar himself. If he spoke of suffering, it was not an abstraction—he walked barefoot and hungry in the snow.

We see then why St. Francis loved Brother Juniper. The dear fool had that type of mind—only he was in the primary department. Literally to give up all, that was easy to his logic. But the story goes that if a sick man asked him for a pig's trotter, he might go off with a knife and cut the trotter from a live pig— too swift from the premise to the conclusion! If he were asked to prepare a great feast, well, did not a great feast consist of fowls and meat and potherbs and eggs? Therefore with logical literalness he put them—shells and feathers and all—into one big pot. What would you? Such men are dangerous in an age when words usually mean other and less than they say.

There is that story of the Father General who roared out so harshly against poor Juniper for taking the silver bells and giving them to a poor woman, that he became quite hoarse. This hoarseness was what Brother Juniper realized and not his own humiliation, and in the dead of night he took the Father

General a bowl of hot and prophylactic porridge. Whereat the General bawled at him for a base fellow and a caitiff. Then the veritable genius of Brother Juniper revealed itself. He saw the situation literally —this indeed is one of the great sayings of literature: "My father, since you will not eat of this porridge that was made for you, at least do me this favor; hold the candle for me and I will eat it." Hold the candle! Well, of course, they ate the porridge together as brethren.

St. Francis understood all this perfectly. "Would to God, my brethren," he exclaimed, "that I had a whole forest of such Junipers." One is glad to know that the fool was with the saint at his deathbed— probably dropping salt tears into a boiling cabbage, practical to the last. O sancta simplicitas!

Lord, make us who are wise in our own conceit fools for your sake.

CHAPTER 2

Bernard of Quintavalle—the Aristocrat

THOSE WHO THINK that the disciples who flocked to St. Francis were those who had nothing to lose and all to gain; who had lived so long with Poverty that they ceased to gird at her chains; such men as the Robbers of the Hills—may be interested to learn that the first disciple of the saint was a rich man, noble and wise. And far on the path of St. Francis he went.

The story goes that St. Francis desired to converse on Divine things with one of his disciples. This man was kneeling in the silence of a green forest glade rapt in prayer. St. Francis called and called—no answer came. He was ever sensitive to the responses of affection and went away peeved and grieved. But as was his wont, he prayed in a solitary place and besought God to tell him why his friend had not answered. The reply came: "Ought a man to forsake God for his creature? Thy friend was united to me." So St. Francis hurried back to the forest glade and cast himself at his friend's feet, commanding him in holy

obedience to obey his behest. His friend, doubtless
astonished, replied: "Verily, if you in turn obey my
command." Then St. Francis said: "In order to
punish my arrogance and rashness you shall now,
even as I lay supine, set one foot on my neck and one
on my mouth crying, 'Lie there, churl, whence comes
such pride to you that thou art so vile a creature?'"
This was hard for the disciple to do, but he did it,
afterwards saying, "In turn I command you by holy
obedience, that every time we are together you rebuke
and correct me harshly for all my faults." Thereafter men wondered at the reverence, love and humility St. Francis used towards his disciple.

This friend was Bernard of Quintavalle, the "first-
born son" of St. Francis.

Now, Bernard was an older man than St. Francis,
and in a worldly sense, a wiser man. He was of a
noble order and possessed great wealth. How came
such a man to vow himself to one who had married
Lady Poverty? It is an illustration of the truth that
too often men cannot hear what we say for the
thunder of what we are. In a day when doing is
elevated above being, reflect that it was the silent
and invisible radiation from the spirit of St. Francis
that brought about the conversion of Bernard. Like
so many rich men he was discontented with life and
hungered for the plain bread of God. He had watched
St. Francis for two years, watched with his quiet wise

eyes how the saint bore humiliation and persecution without his joy in Christ being dimmed or his foot faltering. So Bernard invited St. Francis to lodge with him and planned to share the same room, in which a light ever burned, that perchance he might learn the secret of his holiness. St. Francis noted the design and feigned sleep. When he thought Bernard was at last deep in slumber, he rose and began to pray— prayed with bitter tears of penitence until the grey light of dawn glimmered at the window panes, and crying, "My God, my God."

The light dawned in a double sense on the awed soul of Bernard. He had learned the secret. The Holy Spirit changed his heart. Boldly he spoke: "Brother Francis, I have fully determined to forsake the world." Just like that, as our young folk say. The Holy Spirit, when he authentically works, leaves no room for ifs and buts and philosophic speculation and reference to text books of psychology and debates on theology. "I have fully determined"—that is the language of the Holy Spirit. Conversion, from St. Paul to Brother Bernard, was sudden and sound, as our Methodist friends will be glad to note.

The two friends went to Mass at the bishop's house, and St. Francis opened the Mass book in the name of Jesus Christ. Thereupon appeared these words, "If thou wilt be perfect, go and sell what thou hast and give to the poor and follow me." Two other openings

yielded the Divine commission to the disciples. Thereupon Bernard, fully confirmed, sold his great possessions and with infinite joy gave all to "widows and
orphans, to prisoners and hospitals and pensioners."

Reading the story of St. Francis, we gain the impression that all through he leaned heavily on this
wise quiet man, older than he, and who had been
initiated by a more exhaustive sacrifice than even the
saint himself. For it is recorded that St. Francis was
wont to say of him "that he was worthy of all reverence and had founded this order, for he was the
first who had forsaken the world, holding nothing
back but giving all to Christ's poor; and the first who
began his evangelic poverty by offering himself naked
to the arms of the Crucified, to whom be all praise
and glory without end. Amen."

Brother Bernard was a shining light to the other
disciples. Often he was ravished up to Heaven in
prayer and returning dazed with vision and joy would
cry: "O friars, there is no man in this country, were
he ever so noble, but if he were promised a beautiful
palace filled with gold would not find it easy to carry
a sack filled with dung in order to win that treasure
so noble." They said of him that like the swallows he
soared high by contemplation. Witty Friar Giles hit
it off by saying, *"He feeds flying!"* And he and St.
Francis would often repair to the silence of the woods
rapt in God the whole night long.

At the end, when Bernard lay a-dying, it was
Brother Giles who cried: "Sursum corda, Brother
Bernard, sursum corda." And we may be sure that
Bernard lifted up his heart, for his soul was already
ravished by the vision of that palace of God. He had
thrown all away and was now to receive the immortal
riches of the blessed life. Happy is Bernard, the first-
born Son of St. Francis. *He feeds flying!*

CHAPTER 3

Friar Giles—the Unobtrusive

I DID NOT CHOOSE the blessed Friar Giles for number three of the Friends of St. Francis. He just walked in. Not that he insisted on being number three, for the verb "to insist" was always declined by him; he simply looked at you and you did it. He put the most profound, abstruse and complicated propositions to you with an innocent wide-eyed look, and it was as lucid as water dripping from the bucket of a well.

No, I did not want Friar Giles for number three. He did not provide these jolly human stories of intimate comradeship with St. Francis that I was looking for. Probably that was because St. Francis instantly beheld in him a classic recruit destined for wider spheres than the fresh imprints of his master's bare feet. But as I was reading about him in order to provide myself with arguments why he should be left over—he began to talk; and I was undone. You know how he always began: "Look now, my dearest, it is very truth . . ."

73

There you have it! These saints of most holy humility are terrible gate-crashers. They do not bang on the door or ring, but the door quietly swings open. Jesus must have smiled when he said to Giles, "Knock and it shall be opened to you," for he knew that Giles, that most humble friar, was already stealing into his Sacred Heart.

One of the most startling metaphors in the literature of saintliness is the saying of Friar Giles: "Methinks humility is like a thunderbolt; for even as the bolt makes a terrible crash, breaking, crushing and burning all that it finds in its path, and then nought of that bolt is found, so, in like manner, humility smites and scatters and consumes every wickedness and every vice and every sin; and yet is found to be nought in itself." Humility smites! And is nought! Is there any saying regarding the virtues more profound than this?

St. Francis obviously placed a high value on Giles. When, on his conversion, he fell on his knees on the ground before St. Francis, the saint said, "Dearest Brother, God has wrought in you a very great grace . . . God has chosen you for his knight and most beloved servant." He led him to Friar Bernard and cried: "Our Lord and Master hath sent us a good friar." And journeying to procure cloth for Giles's habit he confided: "Son, my order shall be like the fisher who casts his net into the water and takes a multitude of fishes; and the big fish he holds, and puts the little ones back into the waters." The big fish he holds! St. Francis held Friar Giles.

Yet, was Friar Giles often with St. Francis? All through the story you read things like this: "Friar Giles, by leave of St. Francis, went to St. James the Great in Galicia . . . Friar Giles by leave of St. Francis, went to visit the holy Sepulchre of Christ . . . Friar Giles being in a friary at Rome . . . Friar Giles, when dwelling with a cardinal . . . Friar Giles went out of Rome to the top of a high mountain and found there a deserted church . . . a good man at prayer when Friar Giles died saw his soul come out of Purgatory and ascend to Heaven; and he beheld Jesus Christ come forth to meet the soul of Friar Giles . . ."

Friar Giles always seemed to be away on some great journey, by leave of St. Francis.

I cannot find that Friar Giles ever said very much about his master and exemplar. Yet all the eloquence of the *Little Flowers* does not equal the oratory of the simple fact that Friar Giles moulded his very soul in the soul of St. Francis, was the perfect mirror of St. Francis, spoke with his accent, saw with his eyes.

> "I will speak thy speech, love,
> Think thy thought."

Over and over again when reading his sayings, I have had to turn back to see if this were Friar Giles or St. Francis speaking. *Little Flowers* gives some of his notable sayings, and they are as notable as the sayings of a Kempis in the *Imitatio Christi*. Except maybe they are bolder in metaphor and use more of the rough edge of the speech of the common man.

"How grievous a sinner so ever a man may be, let him not despair while he yet lives, of the infinite mercy of God; for there is no tree in this world so full of thorns, nor so knotted, nor so gnarled, but that men cannot plane it and polish it and adorn it, and make it fair to look upon." Was it a carpenter to whom he was speaking?

"He that would gain and possess perfect peace and rest, must needs account every man his superior . . . Holy humility knows not how to prate." Can we guess the kind of man to whom he spoke these words?

"My dearest," said Giles to a religious who was feeling sore about his superior, "the more you murmur, the heavier the weight of the burden. How useful is the nature of the horse! No matter how swiftly the horse runs, he yet lets himself be ruled and guided, and leaps hither and thither according to the will of the rider. And so likewise ought the servant of God to do, to wit, he should let himself be ruled, guided, turned aside, and bent according to the will of his superior or of any other man, for love of Christ."

"A worldly proverb said 'Never set an empty pot on the fire hoping your neighbor will fill it,' and so God wills that no grace be left empty; for the good God never gives a grace to any man that it be kept empty."

"When a man would work evil, he never asks much counsel for the doing thereof, but many folk seek much counsel and make long delay ere they do good." Many folk? You and I and all of us!

"I would rather live in the world and hope and desire unceasingly and devoutly to enter the religious life, than be clothed in the habit of the holy religious without the practice of virtuous works." The audacity of these giants of humility!

Finally we find him harking back to St. Francis, the never forgotten: "Friar Giles said the ant was not so pleasing to St. Francis as other living things, because of the great diligence she has in gathering together and storing up, in the time of summer, a treasure of grain for the winter, but he was wont to say that the birds pleased him much more, because they laid not up one day for the next." Glory be to holy improvidence! Blessed St. Francis, I am so tired of being told to go to the ant!

And so Friar Giles comes in here because he throws a light back on to St. Francis. He reveals the positive force of humility. Humility is looked upon as a negative virtue, but Friar Giles knew its dynamic shatter-

ing power. It thunders off the doors of Heaven; it
will not be afraid of the trumpets on the day of judgment.

Humility is begotten by the utter prostration of
prayer. Said Friar Giles: "Methinks the high grace
of contemplation is a Divine flame and a sweet emanation of the Holy Ghost, a rapture and an exaltation of the mind which is inebriated in the contemplation of that ineffable savor of Divine sweetness
—a burning inward sense of celestial and unspeakable
glory."

And in that spirit Friar Giles passed away and the
giants and heroes and inheritors of the earth came
proudly to meet him. Among whom would surely be
Friar Bernard to whom Friar Giles had cried in the
hour of death, "Sursum corda, Friar Bernard, sursum
corda." I dream that as the shining ones beheld the
soul of Friar Giles gliding timidly, wonderingly, towards them, they laughed, joyously shouting: "How
now, Friar Giles, sursum corda, sursum corda!"

CHAPTER 4

Friar Masseo—the Gentleman

AN ASTONISHING ASPECT of the influence of St. Francis over his disciples was that in spite of his imposition of a terrible rigidity of rule and of an absolute surrender of pride to humility, he yet called out of each of them a richer individuality. Brother Juniper was naturally a fool and under St. Francis he became a bigger fool than ever. But his foolery was transmuted; he became Christ's fool and made the disciples laugh, because he took Christ so literally. The Lady Clare was not less Clare because she was shorn of her golden hair and wed to poverty. Her loveliness flowered into the loveliness of a handmaiden of the Lord, lily-lovely, and she became the spiritual mother of a thousand daughters. Friar Giles, the wise, dry, slightly cynical philosopher, became more so after his conversion, but the keen edge of his wit punctured only pretension and pride, and in him the high grace of contemplation became a divine flame and a sweet emanation of the Holy Ghost.

Brother Bernard, the nobleman so wise in the wisdom of this world, became unmistakably an ambassador of Christ and the philosopher friend of St. Francis.

Now this is the opposite of what logic would expect and say. Crush individual pride and ambition, clothe with a meager uniform, impose a monotonous rule, and of course you create regimented automata. But it is not so with Christ. He breaks us into bits that he may re-mould us to his heart's desire. But they are the same bits. He answers the prayer which every man prays at least once in his life, "Oh, that a man would arise in me, that the man I am would cease to be." It was not of course the obvious Peter who denied his Lord; Christ founded his Church on the bedrock reality of the Peter whom God knew. Paul became supremely Paul after he had been stricken down on the road to Damascus. It is Sin which damns men into uniformity; it is the Evil One who creates slavish automata. Christ's supernatural grace releases the individuality of a man—in it man becomes what God meant him to be.

This is a long introduction to Friar Masseo; but then he is a good case in point. By nature he was "handsome, stately, and gifted with speech." Left to nature he would have become a *bon viveur,* the pet of society, a social lion; and women would have called him charming and, you know, so witty. But utterly surrendered to the rule of St. Francis, Masseo became really Masseonic. I feel that St. Francis was rather proud of his handsome disciple. Indeed he was enormously amused by Masseo's success in begging. On the way to the land of France, they came to a city sorely hungry. St. Francis begged in one street, Masseo in another. When they set the harvest out on a stone, St. Francis guffawed over the obvious fact that his own mean appearance had elicited only meager and begrudged crusts, while Masseo's handsome mien and charming loquacity had reaped a harvest of whole loaves. "We are not worthy of so great a treasure," St. Francis explained—was there a hint at Friar Masseo's pride? Who then was handsome, who then eloquent? For the fire came into St. Francis and his body burned with beauty and he was shaken with eloquence as he preached upon Poverty and was caught up to Heaven and St. Peter and St. Paul conversed with him. And Masseo feeling mean and small and dumb, felt so strong a flame of love emanate from St. Francis that he was cast a spear's length. Masseo could woo earthly bread; St. Francis royally feasted on God's manna.

One can sense that St. Francis was especially fond of the "handsome, stately, and eloquent" Masseo. He prayed much with him, revealed to him heavenly secrets. Above all he never ceased to test him and try him and elevate him by grinding down his pride. Faithful are the wounds of a friend, and whom St.

Francis loved he wounded. He made something of a fool of Masseo, on one occasion commanding him to turn around and around as a kind of casting for the right road, until poor Masseo tumbled over with vertigo, only to be told calmly that the direction in which his face was pointing must be the right road!

St. Francis, say the *Fioretti,* "desiring to humble Friar Masseo, in order that by reason of the many gifts and graces that God had bestowed on him he should not be puffed up with vainglory." Well, to put it bluntly, St. Francis made him head cook and bottlewasher of the community. In short, he asked Masseo to take on the offices of door-keeper and cook and almoner in order forsooth that his companions might have more time for contemplation! The handsome face was bowed within the cowl, the stately form stooped in obedience, the charming eloquence was silenced in holy acceptance of a command. But soon this became too much for his brethren, and they begged St. Francis to release Masseo from such duties. This of course, was what St. Francis had foreseen. He must have smiled to himself at the success of his guile. Masseo, his beloved disciple, had been enriched by a salutary lesson, and all that Masseo said was, "Father, whatsoever you lay on me, either all or part, that I hold to be wholly done of God." So St. Francis was filled with joy and preached a wonderful sermon on holy humility. Thus his love worried Masseo into greater perfection.

So Masseo lived to a ripe and goodly age. And as his handsome face became finely lined by holy austerity, as his stateliness became more gentle with the courtesies of God, as his eloquence became disciplined to heavenly praise, the deep set and current of his being craved in prayer, to the point of fasts and vigils and bitter tears, for the supreme virtue of humility. So one day Christ called him and said, "What would you give to possess the grace you ask?" Friar Masseo replied, "Lord, I would give the eyes out of my head." The Lord answered, "Have this grace and your eyes also." And therefore Masseo was ever blithe of heart, so blithe that his loquacity sank to a soft cooing like that of a happy dove in a woodland glade. And as such habits do in aging men, this annoyed Friar James of Falterone, who snapped: "Why not change your tune sometimes?" Thereupon Masseo turned his glad countenance and jocund heart to his brother and murmured: "He that has contentment in one song, has no need to change his tune." But beyond death, God put a new song into his mouth.

St. Clare—Maiden Betrothed

"Dear, dead women! With such hair too!
    What's become of all the gold
Used to hang and brush their bosoms?
    I feel chilly and grown old."

In the romanticism of youth I used to find the most Wilhelm Meister-like pathos in the lines written by Browning in his "Toccata of Galuppi's." Whenever I met a girl who was what my boys called a blonde, I used to mutter, "What's become of all the gold?" And if she were very fair to behold, I would add a bit of Shakespeare: "Golden lads and lasses must, like chimney sweepers, come to dust."

But when I took Franciscus as my baptismal name, I learned of a lady whose golden hair is immortal and shines in Paradise. In the old chapel of St. Giorgio we may gaze upon her body garbed in a coarse brown habit, with wild thyme, strewn around her by her sisters seven centuries ago, still holding a lingering fragrance—the Lady Clare, St. Clare, "little plant"

of St. Francis, founder of the order and sisterhood of
Poor Clares. Those who are more eager to expound
the theory of psychiatry than the psychiatrists themselves, airily tell us that in order to eliminate untoward
elements in a person's character, we must search out
and bring to light those of his experiences which hid
themselves in the dark cellar of the Unconscious anon
to emerge to influence and distort his mind. It is
possibly a caricature to explain that a girl has become
a shop-lifter because when she was five she was
frightened by a red-headed man. But in the theory
so crudely stated, there is a manifest confusion—to
the Christian at least. To him it seems that if the
word of the healer is to have curative power, he must
penetrate to that ultimate soul which God created
and not fumble with those accretions of experience
which are more shallow than his soul. To find the
secret of a house, one does not poke about in the
garbage can outside the scullery door but penetrates
to the innermost chambers where the tenant dwells.

This may sound unfair, but as I study the records
of the saints, I do not know that God tactfully adapts
himself to the idiosyncrasies of a man's character, but
makes his call to the man's fundamental soul. The
man is an individual but the call is universal. It is
in the language understood by the created soul. "My
sheep hear my voice." Thus in the story of St. Francis.
I cannot find that he varied or adapted his call. He

spoke the one message to the deeps of the soul—
whether to the outlaws of the hills or to the lawyer;
whether to the rich merchant or to the poor peasant
Giles; whether to the Soldan of Egypt or to the
young and beautiful Clare, daughter of the patrician
houses of Scifi and Fiumi.

Clare, the like of whom there are many today!
Lovely, petted belike, flattered surely, with sweet
aureoled head full of youth's intoxicating dreams,
dreaming of lovers gallant and gay, confident in her
power over men. And so we have to be careful and
diplomatic with them; make the Church attractive
to them, the Faith easy to them, assume they must
have their sweet will. St. Francis never dreamed of
such ways. He never spoke with two voices. He
called for the utter and joyous surrender of the robbers' violence, the careerism of the lawyer, the for-
tune-building of the merchant—and the golden hair
of the Lady Clare. Thus God called to the ever pure
Mary, and to that other Mary who in penitence wept
over the feet of Jesus, and to Lady Clare the lovely
eighteen-year-old aristocrat. Each replied "Ecce,
ancilla Domini," as to the manner born. God knows
hearts better than psychiatrists know them.

St. Francis, moreover, made no bones about the
rights of parents over the immortal souls of their
children. Lady Clare fled like a homing dove from
her parents' mansion on the night of Palm Sunday,

March 18, in the Lent of 1212. Francis awaited her
at the Porziuncola. What had passed between them
God alone knows but Francis was well content that
all was good and right. She fell in the utter silence
of wordless prayer before the altar, took the vows of
poverty, chastity and obedience. As St. Francis had
done before, she threw contemptuously aside her rich
robes and donned coarse sackcloth. She had pride
in the transmutation of a jeweled belt into a rope, of
silken hose into rough wooden sandals, and then
made for any woman the greatest sacrifice of all—she
let St. Francis with his own hands shear away her
golden crown of hair. The shorn head was covered
with a black veil.

St. Francis established the gently nurtured girl in
a few rough cells made with his own hands. It came
to pass that Pope Innocent III (1215) and Honorius
III (1219) approved the rule of Lady Clare's order,
which became the blessed Order of Poor Clares. For
forty years she ruled her Sisters (one of whom was
her own sister Agnes) under the direction of Saint
Francis. Ecce, ancilla Domini!

The friendship between St. Clare and St. Francis
is of another world in its purity of love. It provided
Francis with what all leaders need—the gentle in-
tuitive wisdom of the woman. In an age which held
the subjection of woman as a social law, he treated
her as an equal. Equal pay for equal work! The

guerdon of having nothing—but all of God. His
attitude to her was compact of fatherhood and manhood's chivalry. In Milton's words:

"... When I approach
Her loveliness, so absolute she seems,
And in herself complete, so well to know
Her own, that what she wills to do or say,
Seems wisest, virtuousest, discreetest, best."

It was her prayers he sought when he wavered as
to the call to a universal mission.

Yet reading between the lines one perceives that
he realized that women must be guarded with meticu-
lous chivalry. The Lady Clare petitioned that she
might break bread with him. St. Francis held aloof.
It was only the importunity of his companions that
melted his resolution. Said he, "Since it seems good
to you, even so it seems good to me ... for long has
she been shut up in St. Damian's, and it will profit
her to behold the friary of St. Mary, where her hair
was shorn and she became the spouse of Jesus Christ;
there will we break bread together in the name of
God." Joyfully Clare hastened to the feast, but before saluting her spiritual father, she worshipped at
the altar of the Virgin Mary, at which her golden
hair had fallen. Then St. Francis set forth a meal on
the bare ground. But at the very first course Saint
Francis began to discourse ravishingly of God—the
dear, blessed, simple saints then forgot all about the

longed-for repast but were fed by manna from heaven.

One of the few occasions when St. Francis was roused to indignation—oh, why not say, lost his temper—was, significantly, when a certain friar desired "too gladly" to visit a convent of Poor Clares. Francis scourged him with the whip of words. In short "increpavit eum sanctus durissime, verba non modo referenda inculcans." To make a shot at translation—"he dressed him down in words (as crime reporters say) unfit for publication."

Yet it was another lady, the noblest lady of Rome, the Lady Giacoma, who visited him at his deathbed. When St. Clare and her companions saw his quiet body they cried: "Father, father, what shall we do?" Some poet or other has written:

"All loved and lovely women dear to rhyme,
    Thais, Cassandra, Helen, and their fame,
Burn like tall candles through forgotten time."

Why not add Cleopatra and Nell Gwynne? Pitiful, smoky candles! To us like a star shines the name of Mary—and as a lesser star, the name of Clare. Their names come to us like music stealing over a bed of violets—frankincense and myrrh for Mary; and for Clare—wild thyme!

St. Clare—the Poor Clare

BUT I SEE I must write more of St. Clare, for I have come across a delicious sentence written in an otherwise admirable study of St. Francis by the industrious Mrs. Margaret Oliphant. Writing of the reception into the Franciscan order of the eighteen-year-old Lady Clare, daughter of the Count Scifi, she says it was *"an incident which we can hardly record with satisfaction."*

Across the century we hear the faint "Tut! Tut!" of a Puritanism which had grown weak in principles and strong in prejudices. G. K. Chesterton, with his rapier, as was its wont, flashing to the heart of the subject, remarked, "If it had been really a romantic elopement and the girl had become a bride instead of a nun, practically the whole of the modern world would have made her a heroine. If the action of the Friar towards Clare had been the action of the Friar towards Juliet, everybody would be sympathetic with her exactly as they sympathize with Juliet." (We note in passing that Shakespeare made Juliet's age fourteen; Clare was eighteen.) In that case we may add, Clare would have become a medieval Dorothy Vernon of Haddon Hall, whose romantic elopement with John Manners is still a thrilling legend in Derbyshire, but whose romance is depressed by the sight in a neighboring church of a whole row of effigies of her children who died in infancy.

It is difficult of course to understand Clare. To sacrifice her golden youth at the altar and to become a nun—what a waste! Waste of what? But if a woman foregoes marriage in order to devote herself to an educational career, how honored she is in her community! Yet if the same woman had dedicated her life to the service of God—teaching children, let us say—and had become a nun—what a waste! Waste of what? The one devoted herself to the honors of a career; the other dedicated herself without hope of earthly reward, to the service of God. But of course there are a million and a half more women than men in this country.

But imagine what Hollywood would make of that scene on the night of Palm Sunday, March 18, 1212, more than 700 years ago! We should see the romantic country road in Italy looking, by means of clever technicolor, silver white beneath the Paschal moon. We should see the flicker of torches among the trees, and hear the chant of a waiting band of friars. There would be a flash on a romantic looking St. Francis and then behold! a lovely young aristocratic girl, breathless with escaping through a breach in the walls of her father's castle and with running through the woods . . . she falls at the feet of the friar, and then the scene at the altar when St. Francis takes the shears and the golden hair falls to the floor! We may depend that Hollywood would provide all the atmosphere of an elopement and none of the filmgoers would view it with Oliphantian dissatisfaction.

For truly, as G. K. Chesterton says, it was an elopement. The girl was indeed to become a radiant bride. There were all the elements of an elopement—an eager joyous girl who had heard a voice that subdued her heart and pierced her conscience, the stern forbidding father, the weeping sister Agnes, the escape beneath a silver moon, the red glow of the torches revealing the place of tryst, and a marriage at the altar at last. And the bridegroom was perpetual Poverty, the bridegroom was our Savior Jesus Christ. There was no golden wedding ring, but golden hair shorn; no rich bridal attire, but the cloak of mean cloth.

But, praise God, here was an elopement and a marriage with a happy ending. Like a fairy tale— with a happy ending.

Dear God, what a waste! But the story of St. Clare

is the story of one marriage with a happy ending. For forty-one years St. Clare remained true to her Bridegroom. For forty-one years she so lived and served that she lifted the women of the world into a new and honorable place in society. From her sanctuary in Assisi "there breathed," certifies a biographer, "a very exhalation of purity affecting as a sweet and gracious influence even to chance passersby." Pope Innocent IV stood by her deathbed to give her plenary absolution for all her sins.

"Would to God," he cried weeping, "that my soul had the small need that yours has for this last absolution."

Dear foolish old Friar Juniper, whom St. Clare had nick-named "the plaything of God," came to her deathbed with tears coursing down his face. To him she whispered, "Brother Juniper, have you not some good news to tell me of our God?" Thus with radiant spirit she died August 12, 1253. No red flickering torches welcomed her to this last tryst. But there was the brightness of our blessed Lady Mary.

What kind of a woman was this St. Clare? The picture of her personality is painted with dramatic lucidity in the story of her elopement. We perceive a vivid eager-minded, eager-hearted girl combining in a rare combination strong, even romantic, sentiment, with an indomitable will, which overrode opposition to her sacrificial intent. She possessed this hallmark of the authentic saint—a soft heart and a hard head, sentimentality and shrewdness. St. Clare possessed the impulsiveness of a girl, a Juliet, but her emotion was guided by her will to the goal her soul desired.

St. Clare was a single-minded woman. "Blessed are the pure in heart, for they shall see God." The Greek of the phrase "pure in heart" relates rather to single-mindedness than to sexual purity. St. Clare was from the first the "ancilla Domini." St. Francis was to her the angel of the annunciation of a call to devote herself utterly to God and she conceived the child of the second order of St. Francis. There was no poignancy in her farewell to her girlhood, no "last, long lingering look behind" of the timid novitiate. She literally sprang to the call with a clear joyance, and that single-minded joy never deserted her. She greeted every new sister as one who might possess (as she asked of dear foolish Fr. Juniper) some good news of God. The fragrant courtesy and heart-subduing gentleness for which she and her order were loved, were the flowers that adorned a steady, unwavering will.

St. Clare remained loyal to her one love, her first love; she found her womanhood once and for all. The modern mind believes that it is better to travel than to arrive. It seeks, but does not desire to find, it knocks and hurries away to another door. The modern mind is like a prodigal son, who becoming bored, travels not home again but to another exciting far country. St. Clare sought and found; she knocked and entered the opened door; she turned again home and at home she remained. It is the experience of those who alas, unlike St. Clare, enter the Holy Catholic Church after long questing, saying, "Too late have I loved thee." They have the consciousness of having come home, and envy St. Clare who found home in the golden springtime of her unspoiled girlhood.

This made for a clear mind and a strong will. She never dreamed of deserting the austerity of her initial vow. St. Francis gave her the rule for the second order. It was the same as that of its Brothers, save that the missionary life was not enjoined. She took this rule to herself as a final command, an unquestioned dogma. When St. Francis pointed out to her the hardship of the rule, she answered in wide-eyed innocence, "Are there not other compensations?" When he said, "Be ready, if at any time it be needful to send you to another home." She replied, "I am at all times ready to go wherever you may send me."

A Ruth of the middle ages! When Pope Gregory, on his way to Assisi to prepare for the canonization of St. Francis, visited St. Clare, he gently urged the wisdom of relaxing her vow of poverty. "Holy Father", she replied, "absolve me from my sins, I

have no desire for a dispensation from following
Christ". No wonder that she became a counselor
to St. Francis and gave him courage when he faltered.

For her recreation St. Clare spun thread and made
exquisite altar cloths. She tended a little garden
of "roses and carnations, lavender and rosemary with
other sweet herbs". The hard, bare austerity of her
vow of poverty she graced with delicate art and the
loveliness and fragrance of God's flowers. Thus we
know that, like our blessed Lady Mary, she retained
the grace of her womanhood to the end. Ecce, ancilla
Domini!

CHAPTER 6

Friar Elias—the Politician

"THE LITTLE FLOWERS" takes a poor view of Friar Elias. One hears the undertone of those bitter controversies which rent the order after the molten lava of pristine enthusiasm began to cool and harden. One body of Franciscans, the spirituali, stood by the last Testament of St. Francis. They believed in verbal inspiration. Another body, the conventuali, supported the effort of the Hierarchy to integrate the Franciscan order and the normal discipline of the Church. The spirituali were in danger of becoming mere fanatics. The conventuali were in danger of becoming unadventurous conformists. The extremists of both parties lost the spirit of St. Francis and brought grievous heresy and martyrdom to the order. The schism within the order could not be healed by any act of discipline or legal enactment. It was one of those controversies which cannot be concluded by head-on argument. The order had to reach a life which transcended the barren dichotomies of logic. Today we no longer think in terms of the spirituali and conventuali; we think only of St. Francis.

History makes us all philosophical and wise. Could you expect men who had found life and vision in St. Francis and who clove to him in passionate adoration, to view the Franciscan order with calm philosophy? Our hearts go out to the spirituali; our minds respect the conventuali. The Church had slowly and steadily to bring heart and mind into unison.

What we see now—alas, full late do we see it—is that no single movement, however glorious its vision and beneficent its effects, can constitute the full orb of the truth of the Church. We begin to recognize that enthusiasms left undisciplined, become fissiparous. Enthusiasm naturally proliferates. When the first British Labor government assumed power, America was told that Britain had lit a revolution in the domestic hearth. It is the task of the Church to keep the fires of new enthusiasms confined to the domestic hearth of the House of Faith.

St. Francis experienced in himself well-nigh the whole of Christian influence. The one element he was not called upon to experience was the starlit philosophy of the Church which divinely harmonized Reason, Heart and Will, the trinity of human personality. The metaphysics of the Angelic Doctor would have been Greek to him. But he understood

the lyric of a world awakening to the song of a
bird. He understood physical pain. When the surgeons
were about to draw the red-hot iron across his dim
eyes, he gave that cry which Chesterton described
as one of the masterpieces of "the art of life":
"Brother Fire, God made you beautiful and strong
and useful; I pray you be courteous with me". He
understood spiritual agony; the stigmata were the
visible evidence of it; but La Verna's agony was
the agony of repentance and inspiration; it was a
Gethsemane, but not the Gethsemane of Christ. The
Church is the Body of Christ; no one man and no
one movement can constitute the whole body. The
Church has only one Christ. We recognize this. Let
us not blame the spirituali and conventuali for not
seeing it. We are mercifully free from the blinding
dust of controversy.

The Little Flowers is most naive in its bias against
Friar Elias, but it has the magnaminity to record
his cries in his soul's uttermost despair.

In spite of the stories, Elias was indeed a friend
of St. Francis; the saint was his father and mother.
With the swift keen insight of a saint, Francis doubtless recognized in him the superb organizer and the
audacious statesman. Friar Elias had his own stern
austerity and incurred, one imagines, the unpopu-
larity of the hard task master. The "gossiping diarist"
made a significant passing remark: "The aforesaid

Elias held the provincial ministers so under his rod
that they trembled before him as a reed buffeted by
the waves, or as a lark trembles when the pursuing
hawk is swooping down upon her. Sub dominio
suo durissimum erat vivere—under his rule it was
hardship to live."

The story which is related of how St. Francis had
a dream in which Friar Elias was indicated as
"damned" and doomed to die outside the order, is
a story that puzzles the student. Had the dream an
objective validity? The psychologist might guess that
the source of it was the troubled mind of the saint,
troubled over the friar's tendency to prosaic con-
solidation of a movement that began in song. Yet
even so, Friar Elias comes out not badly. The proud,
stern statesman showed a marvelous humility before
the dire rebuke of one he revered. The story goes
that the saint began to shun the friar and that Elias,
perturbed, asked the reason. I am compelled to make
a long quotation: "And St. Francis answered, 'it
has been revealed to me by God that you, for your
sins, shall become a runagate and shall die outside
the order; and God has likewise revealed to me
that you are damned'. Hearing these words, Friar
Elias spake thus, 'My reverend father, I pray for
the love of Jesus Christ that you shun me not, nor
cast me from you, but as a good shepherd, after the
example of Christ, seek out and receive again the

sheep that will perish except you aid him, and that you will pray to God for me, if haply he may revoke the sentence of my damnation; for it is written that God will remit the sentence if the sinner amend his ways; and I have such great faith in your prayers, that if I were in the midst of Hell, and you prayed to God for me, I should feel some refreshment; wherefore yet again I beseech you to commend me, a sinner, unto God, who came to save sinners, that he may receive me to his mercy-seat'. Friar Elias said this with great devotion and tears; whereat saint Francis, even as a compassionate father, promised he would pray for him".

And mark the end of the story. When Elias became a rebel to the Church tempted by his political mind to go king-making, and at last lay dying, a lay brother said to him: "Dearest brother mine, it grieves me sorely that you are excommunicate and cast out of your order, and even so shall die; but if you see any way or means whereby I may deliver you from this peril, willingly will I undertake any toil for you". Friar Elias answered, "Brother mine, no other way do I see but that you repair to the Pope and beseech him for the love of God and St. Francis, his servant, at whose teachings I forsook the world, that he assoil me from his ban and restore to me the habit of the order". And lo! the Pope assoiled Elias and restored the habit to him. And Elias died, his soul salvaged by the merits of Saint Francis and by his prayers, wherein Friar Elias had placed hope so great.

Friar Elias was no Judas. He did not sell St. Francis for pieces of silver. His own rash heart and arrogant mind was his undoing. He was more of a Peter who denied his Lord, and at last the same Lord came to Peter and said "Lovest thou me? Feed my sheep".

CHAPTER 7

The Wolf of Gubbio—Everyman

I THINK WE MUST regard the Wolf of Gubbio as a friend of St. Francis. For one thing the Wolf is the hero of a typical Franciscan story, and for the other there is a symbolic significance in it which reveals the secret of the saint's relationship with all God's creation.

Now the penalty. A saint must pay for performing a miracle, as the rationalist will not allow him to do anything naturally. This is the materialistic dialectic. If a man, on good evidence, has performed one miracle, he is dangerous. Make him perform a thousand, and he is laughable. We may be fond of a "jongleur de Dieu", but a juggler of God is absurd. In short, if you desire to weaken the evidence of the miraculous in a man, you inoculate his story, as it were, with a miracle virus—that is to say, you insist that everything he did was miraculous. That of course turns him into a legend. Thus, for instance, if there be good evidence that a saint changed a stone into a loaf of bread in some desperate emergency, you smother the fact by encouraging a hundred stories, so that a fried egg flies through the air and settles on his plate like a hunter's moon, and grapes grow on an ivy vine as he plays on his fiddle—and so on. Then you smile amusedly and murmur, "What delightful legends! How flowers do grow around these medieval saints! Why, even St. Thomas Aquinas floated in the air—levitation, you know. Amusing, is it not?" In short, hopelessly to mix a metaphor, the rationalist leads us up the garden path in order to tempt us to throw out the baby with the bath water.

Perceive the same technique at Christmastide. We have hidden the manger with the Christmas tree—with gifts for all. No gold and myrrh and frankincense for the Babe, but a toy engine for Tommy. Children are shown fairyland—bright stars wandering, music in the air, Eastern kings astride camels, shepherds adoring, an ox and an ass gazing. St. Francis made his first crib, but we have gone on to make it pretty. Then it is easy to proceed to St. Nicholas and Santa Claus with his reindeer and sack and chimney descents, and so on to Saxon wassail and jolly old carols. Such a proliferating fairy tale that only one fact is hidden away—the central fact that God the Son was born of the Virgin Mary to save mankind from sin.

So take the story of St. Francis and the Wolf.
The fierce old wolf was terrifying the village of
Gubbio. St. Francis went to his lair and talked to
him, and the wolf gave him his paw and shook
hands, and thereafter, like a good Christian, played
with children and became the pet of the village.
Jolly good story! Lovely legend for children! Yet is
this so clever? The children I know prefer the wolf
in Red Riding Hood to the grandmother. But I expect the modern educationalist deprecates this for
fear that some psychiatrist may discover it creates
suppressions and complexes—that in this way a boy
grows up to hate his mother-in-law. I wonder why
Bernard Shaw dramatized the story of Androcles and
the Lion?

But actually I do not regard the story as much
of a miracle, and I smile at the naive attempts of
the intellectuals to build it up from the Taming-of-
Robbers theme. It seems rather a fact within human
experience. The Wolf of Gubbio was neither the first
nor the last to raise a deprecatory and doglike paw
to a human friend. Lord Grey of Falloden created
a sanctuary for wild fowl. They flew down to its
waters and nested and rested and fed without
evincing the slightest fear of man. Yet a few miles
beyond the boundary of the sanctuary there were
other waters. The geese would fly down to these
also but with every sign of alert fear of man. They

knew precisely where the boundary line of the sanctuary lay and within it lost all fear. Inside was the love of Lord Grey of Falloden.

But if the taming of the wolf of Gubbio is not a supreme miracle in itself, it is significant inasmuch as the proffered paw points to what is the essential miracle. St. Francis himself was the miracle. The fact that our Lord gave St. Francis his own power of passing through all barriers that divide man from man, and man from beast—that is the miracle. He walked through bolted doors and captured all imprisoned hearts whether of men or beasts and birds— cruel Saracens, lawless robbers, proud princes, simple fools and the shepherdless common folk.

"He prayeth best who loveth best
    All things both great and small;
For the dear God who loveth us,
    He made and loved them all".

St. Francis recognized in the wolf a typical prisoner. Doubtless the wolf snarled at first. Original sin always snarls at the onset of supernatural grace. But the wolf soon recognized he was known and loved—his bluff called. So he did what dogs naturally do, he proffered a repentant paw as a pledge, and thereafter (as all good Christians do) he played with little children.

But—but is there not a profound significance in the story? As I read it once more, there comes to

me that tremendous searching passage in St. Paul's
Epistle to the Romans (8, 18 to 25; Msgr. R. Knox's
translation): "If creation is full of expectancy, that
is because it is waiting for the sons of God to be
made known. . . . Nature in its turn will be set free
from the tyranny of corruption to share in the glorious freedom of God's sons. The whole of nature,
as we know, groans in a common travail all the
while. We ourselves groan in our hearts, waiting for
the adoption which is the transforming of our bodies
from their slavery".

Msgr. Ronald Knox adds the comment: "The
word here translated creation or created nature, probably means creation as a whole. St. Paul with something of a poetic outlook, sees the struggle for sur-
vival in nature as a proof of the dumb aspiration
towards that more perfect creation which is to come;
the agony of the frustrated striving is the birthpang
of a new order".

And so, read the story of the wolf of Gubbio in
the light of this passage and of this comment. Thus
is pictured the desperate strait of the universe when
the angel of the Annunciation called to Mary and
when the Incarnation and Redemption hung poised
in the will of a woman. Mary chose. Jesus was born
—and she Mater Dei. Jesus passed beyond original
sin and reconciled God and man.

Behind the kindly picture of St. Francis shaking hands with a wolf there looms a Cross—on which our Blessed Savior died—and shook hands with the wolf. Domine, non sum dignus. . . .

Part III

The Third Order

CHAPTER 1

St. Francis at the Wars

THIS CHAPTER is in the nature of a preface to a study of the mission of the Third Order.

It touches on wars and the part St. Francis played in them. All social problems arise from some kind of war between nations and classes. If the spirit in which St. Francis faced the Saracen soldan of Egypt were inspired by a power both universal and immortal, it would be valid for the hatreds and hostilities of today. If it were merely the glow of the romanticism of a saint of medieval Italy, then what has Francis to do with the economic problems of Europe and the threat of war between Soviet Russia and the Western nations? This is written in the faith that the message of St. Francis, and the spirit of the man behind it, is of universal validity. That is precisely why I have protested so much against the sentimentalism that hides St. Francis in a romantic mist of fairy tales. Such a charming man! A gifted lady wrote to me recently: "The book on St. Francis brought back memories of college days when we had a nature study guild delighting in the name of the Guild of St. Francis." There you have it! A delightful activity, no doubt. Love of birds, of course. But I think of the eventide on which St. Francis died. His request that he be stripped of his habit had been obeyed. He lay on the bare ground, the stigmata visible on his hands and feet, and while the suffering of our Savior was being read from the Gospel of St. John, he died. And it is recorded that as he breathed his last, there was "some late lark singing."

Only that St. Francis who made an utter renunciation of material things and of earthly ambitions; only that St. Francis who was inspired with such a burning compassion for all human beings that he reconciled them one to the other wherever he went; only that St. Francis who rebuilt ruined chapels so that the Mass of the eternal sacrifice of God the Son might be celebrated on their altars; only that St. Francis who bore the five wounds of Jesus Christ on his body and who died ungarmented on the naked earth—only that St. Francis, I say, possesses any relevance to the problems of today. Any other St. Francis is as irrelevant to the enormous tragedies of the modern world as Tennyson's Sir Galahad and Sherwood Forest's Robin Hood.

The dominant force in St. Francis was his compassion. Compassion is not a static emotion as its

Greek equivalent "sympathy" may well be. It was a love supernaturally radiant in words and deeds. The outstanding virtue of his compassion was its reconciling influence. It melted hostility to himself, and it made sworn enemies shake hands with each other. Although his way of life constantly challenged powerful interests, it is not recorded that he ever made one enemy. Even his opponents were glad to have his blessing. In the Vatican, where men devised clever and devious ways of gaining the approval of the pontiff, St. Francis walked freely, and no pope refused him. He was unaware of his power. He had no self-consciousness and no vanity. All men were subdued by his compassion.

St. Francis would brook no hatred between man and man. But he did not reconcile them by the direct approach—no didactic finger, no railing argument, no interchange of dialectical notes. Reconciliation took place in the presence of his compassion.

A vivid contemporary picture is painted by Thomas of Spalato. St. Francis visited Bologna in 1222 when he was forty-one years of age. He knew that Bologna needed above all peace between the rival factions who disturbed the city's life. Here are Spalato's own words:

"In the same year, on the day of the Assumption of the Mother of God, when I was a student at Bologna, I saw St. Francis preaching in the piazza

before the Palazzo Publico, where almost the whole
town was assembled. The theme of his sermon was
Angels, Men, Devils. And he spoke so well and so
wisely of these three rational spirits that to many
learned men who were there the sermon of this
ignorant man seemed worthy of no little admiration,
in spite of the fact that he did not keep to the method
of an expositor so much as of an extempore speaker.
Indeed, the whole manner of his speech was cal-
culated to stamp out enmities and to make peace.
His tunic was dirty, his person unprepossessing, and
his face far from handsome; yet God gave such
power to his words that many factions of the nobility,
among whom the fierce anger of ancient feuds had
been raging with much bloodshed, were brought to
reconciliation."

But St. Francis had personal experience of the
wars of his day. His first experience began on a day
when he rode forth, a gay youth of twenty-one, as
a soldier of Assisi in a war against Perugia. Probably it was nothing more that a glorified raid, but
blood was shed and women sorrowed for their slain.
The forces of Assisi were defeated and young Francis
languished as a prisoner of war in a fortress for two
years. It is recorded that even then he changed the
heart of a fellow prisoner whose bitterness troubled
the company.

Francis returned home with the seeds of disease

in his body. But by the time a military expedition
was organized against Apulia, his health and high
spirits had returned. Encouraged by his proud father,
he equipped himself with glittering and costly
accoutrements. But things always happened to
Francis. He felt a sense of shame as he contemplated
the mean habiliments of a companion riding by his
side. It was a typically Franciscan gesture to suggest
that he should exchange his equipment with his fellow soldier. That night he had a vision and a voice
said to him, "Why do you follow the servant instead
of the Master?" Soon after that his father and mother
heard the clatter of a horse's hooves outside their
door. Francis had returned ignominiously from the
war. The significance of the words of the voice had
not yet become clear to him; he was yet to understand that War was the servant and Christ was
the Master.

In 1215 a general council of the Church launched
another crusade for the recovery of the Holy Places.
This was a part of a general plan for a revival of
Christian zeal in the Church Militant. St. Francis
did not seem to be affected by the military crusade,
but he was fired rather by the vision of a crusade
for God's righteousness and holy love. His meet-
ing with a man of like spirit, St. Dominic, served
to increase his zeal, and St. Dominic begged the gift

of the cord which bound the habit of Francis, and tied it around himself.

Yet the very evangelical zeal inspired by the fourth council of the Lateran was to involve St. Francis in the crusade after all. His friars were to become missionaries, he would be a missionary too. With thirteen friars he sailed to Acre, the Christian stronghold, and from thence to Egypt to the front line of the crusading army. What happened then was recorded by one of the crusaders, James de Vitry:

"We saw the founder and head of this order, whom all the others obey as their prior, a simple and ignorant man, but loved of God and men, by name Brother Francis. To such a degree of exaltation and fervor of spirit was he seized that when he had come to the Christian army outside Damietta in Egypt he reached the camp of the Soldan of Egypt himself, so bold was he and so fortified with the shield of faith. When the Saracens captured him on the road, he said 'I am a Christian; lead me to your lord.' And when they had dragged him before the soldan, the cruel beast was turned to gentleness by the expression on the face of the man of God, so that for several days he listened most attentively to his preaching to them the faith of Christ. At length, fearing lest some of his people should be converted to the Lord by the power of his words, and so go over to the Christian army, he ordered him, with all reverence and with every safeguard, to return to our camp, saying to him at the last, 'Pray for me that God may reveal to me that law and that faith which is to him most pleasing!' "

Father Dominic Devas O.F.M., in his brilliant booklet on St. Francis, quotes the above passage and adds the tremendous sentence *"It was the death-blow to the Crusades."* This is a striking, if not stabbing, judgment. As a metaphor it may be too forth-right. Christian leaders were to come after St. Francis who would condone a just war, and all wars may be defined too easily as just. St. Francis confronting the soldan with his compassion did not in fact strike a death-blow at war. He did not lay down a general principle. He did not prate about an impossible pacifism. He was what he was, both to the Christian and to the Saracen forces: the exemplar of a new compassion. He did and said something which sank into the consciousness of the Church and in the long run undermined the belief that spiritual ends can be attained by violence. It is possible that St. Francis would say (although he was not good at abstract argument) that a war in defence of life and liberty was not violence. His conduct, however, did indeed imply that spiritual ends should not be attained by violence, but should be attained only by Christ's quality of love. Whether we apply this to the dark hostility between Russia and the Western nations or to those wars between classes which break out in economic strife, the principle remains the same. Direct violent action, violence either by political force or might of arms, cannot bring lasting peace but only the temporary peace of exhaustion. Only the accepted holy love of God can reconcile man to man.

The perturbed in mind may reply, "Yes, but where is the St. Francis who will confront the modern soldan and uplift his soul by his preaching of God's righteousness and love? In the soldan's camp no abstract general principle was laid down. The righteousness and love of God spoke through a living and unique man. Where is that man?" The answer is just. It would seem that the world has no man of the calibre of St. Francis who is free to take his message to the Kremlin.

But among the statesmen of the nations of the world is there any man who is even trying to be like St. Francis? Or is that an unfair question? Abuse is met by abuse as argument provokes argument. Hatred begets hatred and threats are answered by threats. There is political maneuvering, but no voice of compassion speaks from heart to heart. Where is the reconciling word in the world today? Is no politician in the world able to speak the word which goes deep into the human soul and evokes response? There seems to be no upspringing of generous emotion, none of that spontaneous holding out of friend-

ship's hand as with the lords of Bologna. The world
to the jaundiced eye is imprisoned within its suspicions and hatreds and fears and lusts and pride. It
is the Devil's spell. Who can break the spell?

Even while we ask, another says: "But St. Francis
did no more than fill the soldan with awe. The
soldan was not converted to the Christian Faith: the
crusaders did not throw away their swords. Things
remained as they were. St. Francis returned to Italy."

We remain silent but ponder this. If things remained as they were, then the world would be the
same today if St. Francis had never lived. But we
cannot imagine a world in which St. Francis never
lived. And since St. Francis is a part of the continu-
ing ministry of Christ in his Church, we should have
to go on and assert that it would have made no
difference to the world had Christ never died upon
the Cross. *St. Francis cannot be eliminated from
the conscience of mankind.* Today he moves as a
living force. He speaks the reconciling word but there
is the bleak mystery of the deaf ear and the numb
heart.

So we are driven back to God—to the Holy Spirit
of God given to his Church. That is not despair;
it is faith.

Are we wrong in waiting for another St. Francis?
Does God duplicate his prophets? Stay: is the message to us that our task is to multiply the disciples

of St. Francis, so that within the corporate body of the Third Order St. Francis will live again?

Now, this I have found from self-examination and from gentle observation of other men—that when we seek a remedy for social ills, we demand a policy. A policy conjures up a vision of a group of responsible men able to cure social disease and whom we can blame if they fail. Our enthusiasm for the policy is clamant and we remain blind to the fact that our clamor is a self-righteous eloquence. Do I not wash my hands and say of myself: "I find no fault with this man. The committee is to blame." But as the ocean is fed by rivers and rivers are fed by tributaries, and tributaries are fed by big streams into which rivulets flow, so the world's dark sea of guilt is fed by the bitter drops which seep from our own suspicions, our own small habits and our own timid fears. These contribute to every war that is waged. As George Meredith wrote:

"In tragic life, God wot,
      No villain need be. Passions spin the plot;
      We are betrayed by what is false within."

The truth is there. If each one of us would say, "I am betrayed by what is false within," then penitence would come. Instead of the grandiloquent policy— repentance and prayer. And after such self-humiliation and Christ's cleaning, there would flow into our deeps that compassion which is the radiance of love at peace with God and therefore with man. Quiescently we wait for some great Sun of Peace to shine upon the world. Perhaps God wills it that we light a candle in our own souls.

> "How far that little candle throws it beam,
>
> So shines a good deed in a naughty world."

This then is all I can immediately learn from St. Francis going to the wars; that I myself—*myself!* —must be a center of compassion and peace. We who have been scarred by the years are watching the bewildered youth of today. Do we not find ourselves thinking:

"Would that I had my children about my knees again, so that instead of barren precepts the spirit of compassion and peace might flow from me to them?"

It may chance that a little poem may move us deeply where great ones fail. As I sat silent and brooding before a dying fire, I read verses written by Mildred R. Howland for the Atlantic Monthly— they are reproduced by the gracious permission of the editor and of the writer of them:

> "How shall we teach
> A child to reach
> Beyond himself and touch the stars—
> We who have stooped so much?
> How shall we tell

A child to dwell
With honor, live and die
For truth—
We who have lived a lie?
How shall we say
To him, 'the way
Of life is through the gate,
Of love'—
We who have learned to hate?
How shall we dare
To teach him prayer
And turn him toward the way
of Faith—
We who no longer pray!"

CHAPTER 2

Revelation and Revolution

I am a member of the Third Order of St. Francis. I believe that the teaching of the Third Order has within it the power to solve the social problems that bewilder the world today. St. Francis founded the order in 1221, more than 700 years ago. Its first members were called "Penitents", because they repented of that obsession with material things which had dominated their lives. They were men and women who felt the regenerating power of the saint's teaching but were unable to forsake their responsibilities by adopting the absolute way of poverty. The Lady Giacoma and Count Orlando of Chiusi (who gave Mount La Verna to Francis) and Lucchesio, rich merchant of Poggibonzi, were among the distinguished, but there were thousands of humble folk of like mind. "Whoever", to quote Sabatier's words, "was free at heart from all material servitude and who lived without hoarding", were always true Franciscans. To them St. Francis said: "Make not all

123

haste to leave your home; but stay where you are, and I will show you what to do for the salvation of your souls." Note at once that he did not say, "I will show you what to do to put the world right." If he had thought at all in terms of Utopia, which one doubts, he would have believed that the salvation of the individual soul was the beginning of social reform.

"Stay where you are". That was the curious marching order to the Third Order. "Stay put" is more difficult than "Go rampaging"! Therefore it seems necessary to examine the background of what we may call apostolic social ethics before we can appreciate the significance of the Third Order to the world today.

The apostles knew nothing of "revolution". That is why their attitude to the problems of the relationship between the individual and the social state appears so naive to the modern Utopian. Exasperatingly they took it for granted that if men were right with God then the Society in which they lived would become right. Obviously that was a long-term view. "Revolution in our time" was not their slogan. They thought more about Revelation.

The social background of the New Testament story is the one-man craftsmanship of a carpenter's shop, of landowners with rights over their land, of stewards of property, merchants free to buy and sell, soldiers, magistrates, and civil servants. The place of Christ's birth is determined by a State decree. There is no denunciation of imperial government as such. Jesus sorrows over the rich young man not because he is rich but because he has not the grace to become poor. The owner of the vineyard has the right to pay just wages without permission from outside organization. St. Paul is a scholar but is also a tentmaker, and he is proud of his Roman citizenship. Simon Peter has a notable respect for authority, being anxious to rebut the charge that Christians were revolutionaries; he is also the owner of a small fishing fleet. St. Paul's epistle to Philemon, although it charges a Christian master to receive back a runaway slave in the spirit of Christ, does not indulge in any denunciation of slavery as an institution.

There is no detailed guidance in the New Testament about social problems. It is no text book of blue print plans. It does not mention political economy, democracy, the proletariat, state ownership and hospitals. But the New Testament is aglow with dynamic revolutionary power—in the sense that it is power to transform men and society, and remould the world to the justice of God. Jesus wept over the proletariat as being sheep without a shepherd and offered men a shepherd who would lay down his life for the sheep. He said all there was to say about political economy when he laid it down that our

Heavenly Father knows we have need of food and raiment. There was an implied program for the reformer in his saying, "Seek ye first the kingdom of God and its justice, and all these things shall be added unto you." We well understand the impatience of those who say, "First put your political economy right and Utopia will follow automatically." But Jesus had nothing to say about the rights of man, but everything to say about the rights of God.

The New Testament is all about Revelation and has nothing to say about Revolution. If the gift of the Holy Spirit to the newly founded Church meant anything at all, it meant *influence,* not *power.* It meant the sap rising in springtime, not the atomic bomb. If the Church seeks political power, it weakens its mission. One saint able to renew life is worth a hundred concordats, necessary as concordats may be. Transmutation, not reformation, is the secret of that power. Transmutation comes by the supernatural grace of God. Reformation may be nothing more than tying apples on a sapless tree. Transmutation brings a harvest; reformation Dead Sea apples.

Within a few centuries of the crucifixion of Christ the gladiatorial games were abolished, hospitals established, slavery is made abhorrent to the Christian conscience, womanhood given a new status, marriage (so horribly debased) elevated to a sacrament, children regarded as sacred; and the conception of

a supernatural justice of God began to put the fear
of God into the minds of the lawless. As the soul of
man was given an enormous value, the State was
relegated to second place. The rights of man were
not conferred by the State but were an immediate
and inalienable gift of God. There is a kingship of
Christ that checks the tyranny of earthly rulers. The
Church is an evolutionary church by virtue of the
gift of the Holy Spirit, but it is not to be made
more perfect by democratic legislation. The Church,
like the city of St. John's vision, is let down from
Heaven by God. It is the Body of Christ and needs
no human touch. Its members have a life to live.

I imagine that this was something of the background of truth present in the mind of St. Francis.
Not consciously perhaps, for he was not a theologian
and not a philosopher like St. Thomas Aquinas,
certainly not a reformer either religious or social.
He was not critical of the Church—he accepted its
faith and discipline wholeheartedly. He was not
critical of the social state either. That he was in-
troducing either ecclesiastical or social reform never
entered his head. He moved among princes of the
State and princes of the Church, among aristocrats
and outlaws, among rich men and poor men, with
no regard for any social distinction. He loved individuals intensely with a love born of his passion
for Christ. He saw individuals shackled by the en-

tanglements of material things—he was amazed that
men should miss the heavenly joy which he knew.

Yet he moved popes to wonder and princes to
praise. He lit a new light in the Church and enriched its traditions with an immortal story, and he
gave men a way of life which ever since has made
the fussy Utopian seem prosaic and dull. He put
an idea into the minds of Western civilization which
has never been quenched. After the thunder of Marx
comes the still small voice.

But the princes of his day were not slow to recognize the social significance of his teaching. They were
perturbed by the implications of the Third Order.
They feared for their feudal prerogatives and sought
to strangle the Tertiary movement at its birth. The
Tertiaries held out their hands to Mother Church.
Pope Gregory IX afforded them protection. He in-
structed the bishops to "allow no one to molest the
Tertiaries." Richard Whitwell in his Life of St.
Francis of Assisi went so far as to write: *"Of all
the several shocks which finally broke the power of
the Feudal system few have struck deeper than this
single sentence of the Pope."*

CHAPTER 3

The Dilemma of Civilization

CIVILIZATION is in the grip of the Great Dilemma. And there appears to be no solution to it. The good mankind would do, it does not do, and the evil mankind would not do, that it does. We are becoming exhausted by our efforts to lift ourselves by our own waist-belts. Technical science and economic planning are both waist-belt efforts. Fevered ideologies offer to solve the dilemma; in them we have the curious combination of emotional idealism and the materialism of economic organization. But the hunger of man's soul is not appeased.

How has civilization come to the great dilemma? It is convenient to start with that period of history of which the Reformation was a part. Gunpowder was invented, and the peasant became the equal of the knight on horseback. The telescope was invented, and men who had lived in a little world domed over by a constricting sky became conscious of a universe of infinite space and of planets among which our earth moved in its tiny orbit. Explorers discovered the new world, and Europe was excited by an expanding universe calling to adventure and wealth. Almost at the moment when Medieval culture, economic and religious, seemed to blossom to perfection, it began to disintegrate. Men rent its unity by sword-like interrogations. The Turks captured Constantinople and scholars fled westward with the immortal manuscripts of Greek culture. The new learning sprang from the old philosophies. The human mind was dazzled and confused and blinked in blinding sunlight. The individual emerged. He resented authority; he hungered for self-expression; he heard the arrogant call of the intellect. "Seek and ye shall find." The feudal system was broken, the medieval culture was no longer holding men together in brotherhood, the Church was divided. "Progress," the shallow said. It was not so much progression as a stampede.

But the time came when technical science was able to exploit natural forces. A new principle of organization came into existence. Men organized to produce. It was Carlisle's gospel: Work! Work! Produce! Produce! Coal, steam power, machinery, offered to bring prosperity to appease the hunger of men. The poor souls who with some blind instinct smashed machinery, were told that machinery would release men from the tyranny of labor. But not many men were able to buy machinery. Hungry workers were forced to feed the still more hungry machine. Home industry by crystal streams was swallowed up by "the dark satanic mills". Men, women and children were thrust down into coal mines. Back-to-back houses with no sanitation were built by tens of thousands in cities swelling to overflow. Devastated countryside, ugly towns, stunted people, colossal wealth accumulating in a few hands—thus the Industrial Revolution.

But the soul of man hit back. John Wesley showed in his great evangel that the soul of man could repent and look for the kingdom of God. The black faces of the miners were marked by the white channels of tears as he preached. Much of the degradation was covered up. The Victorians began to convince themselves that there was a fair civilization after all—there was music, art, and literature to guild the scene. William Morris could cry:

"The singers have sung, and the builders have
        builded,
    The painters have fashioned their tales of delight:
For what and for whom hath the world's book been
        guilded,
    When all is for these but the blackness of night?"
But that appeared to be the utterance of an extremist. Bright promises cheered mankind along. Democracy through the vote, free education. John

Bright even offered cheap newspapers. The basic principles of the welfare state were laid down long before the two world wars. Intellectuals and scientists preached ameliorization, humanity was evolving towards the good time—H. G. Wells, George Bernard Shaw and the rest.

But the fundamental evil in the soul of man remained untouched. It must have been untouched. What other explanation is there of the two world wars with their colossal brutality, their slaughter, their inconceivable devastation, their impoverishment of the resources of the world? The Goths were amateurs in devastation compared with this. Nero was a petty sadist; Roman crucifixions were nothing compared with modern concentration camps.

Materialism was the evil. That is an abstract term. Call it greed. Not, of course, conscious greed, but hunger for more goods. Utopia was a place of more goods. The expanding populations of the world demanded more goods. Seek ye first abundant goods and the kingdom of God will be added unto you—as a by-product! The mounting hunger became a frantic greed; jealousy and hatreds and rivalries spawned in the sea of mud. Jeremiahs prophesied; the world was deaf. War broke. Hell was let loose. What was mankind's post-war response? More goods! A fairer life through more goods! Seek ye first more goods. But now the goods will not go round.

Civilization stands in the great dilemma. To understand why it is so, probe into the place where goods are made—the industrial system. Many industries are run along beneficent lines. There are good men at the head of many industries. The State, the repository of all social ideals, is a great employer. That is not the point. It does not affect the great dilemma.

The truth is that the life of man is not an integrated life. Life for the great majority is split in half—one half consists in unwilling labor, the other half in fevered leisure. From this basic fact of a disintegrated life arises our discontent, our profound sense of malaise.

Industry has inevitably evolved the system of mass production. Mass production necessitates repetitive labor. Few men see the whole product for which they labor; all day long they concentrate on one minute part. Craftsmanship has decayed. Men and women make ugly and shoddy things. They say workers like repetitive labor. It dopes the intellect; it is the way of least resistance. Yet instinctively they seek more leisure and more pleasure. But content will not come. It cannot. Life is not integrated. We do not work for the glory of God. If work is ignoble, leisure will be sensual. Nationalization of industries has not even faced the basic spiritual truth. It gives even greater authority to the errors of capitalism.

But that is not all. Mass production necessitates concentrating workers in vast factories and shops. We have evolved enormous aggregations of workers in our cities, a tide of workers on bus and train surge to and fro. This concentration is turning the people into a proletariat. The herd instinct grows stronger. The proletariat becomes more susceptible to suggestion. Its very hunger for more goods and more leisure leads inevitably to stricter organization and control. We become accustomed to regulations. We grow spoon-fed. The radio blares. Suggestions from a hundred causes seep into the soul, deadening its divine faculties. In spite of our determination to avoid the totalitarian state, we are preparing ourselves, our minds, our souls, for a totalitarian way of life. That is the great dilemma.

Is there any solution? Must mankind accelerate its march towards the abyss? Will the ever increasing tempo of our fanaticisms send us rushing down the cliff into the sea? The leader of the Gadarene swine doubtless shouted, "Progress, brothers, progress!"

One thing is certain. Spiritual disease cannot be cured by the *materia medica* of materialism. Spiritual diseases call for spiritual remedies. The body cannot prescribe for the soul. Soul must doctor soul. If mankind is to change the direction of its march, it must experience a change of heart. Men mock us when we say that. They laugh if we cannot produce a plan. The plan of salvation is not a blue print. I know no more of a plan to save civilization from the great dilemma than Peter knew on the day that his denied Lord died on the Cross. I only know that Christ rose from the dead and changed the hearts of men. The Cross was the most practical force in history.

But after all, it is natural for earnest men to ask what they shall do next. Pray, I should reply. But this is a book about St. Francis, and this section deals with the Third Order. We cannot go back. Organized industries cannot be scrapped and cities razed to the ground. The great dilemma calls for the greatest victory of the spirit yet achieved. The total story of the Bible is a parable. Mankind began in a fair garden and ended in a city. Only it was a City of God inhabited by the redeemed. Can the Third Order redeem industry and spiritualize our cities?

CHAPTER 4

Ownership or Stewardship

St. Francis solved the problem arising from man's hunger for material goods by dedicating himself to stark poverty. Not stark for him! He made a romance of it; he wedded Lady Poverty. He personified poverty; it was Holy Poverty. He saw it on the Cross of Christ; he saw it in those pensioners of God, the birds. The gilded youth of Assisi who had ridden forth to the wars in all the glittering panoply of a knight, threw his rich coat at his father's feet and tied coarse sacking about him. He would not own anything, not a penny, not a crust. That was his solution. The social state around him was fundamentally similar to ours in its unrest and spiritual malaise. Feudal disciplines were breaking down, the nobility was cruel and powerful, but a new wealthy mercantile class was arising. Opulence went side by side with poverty. The workers hungered and clamored for bread and goods. "You are all the same," St. Francis said in effect. "Rich or poor you are hungry for material goods. Walk in my way, in which you possess nothing but rejoice in the blessing of holy Poverty." And it looked as if all Italy would flock after him. He was the Pied Piper of Umbria. Men followed his music, food and raiment quite forgotten.

Now, St. Francis was not a visionary, nor the more inept intellectual. He always lunged straight at the heart of things. He was soon made aware that there were those who could not join his order for the simple reason that they were married, and in industry and agriculture held responsible posts. Who made the humble garments the friars wore? Who grew the corn and ground the floor and baked the bread which kind hands gave him? He saw that there were Franciscans by the legion who could never belong to the First or the Second Order. The matter came to a head. A rich merchant of Poggibonzi named Lucchesio had gathered a group of penitents about him. St. Francis saw a vision of untilled fields, of idle mills, of homes left desolate. St. Francis grasped the solution. "Make not all haste," he said, "to leave your homes; *but stay where you are,* and I will show you what to do for the salvation of your souls." G. K. Chesterton referred to the "audacity and simplicity of the Franciscan plan for quartering its spiritual soldiery upon the population." "It was completely successful," he went on. "It was an example of something that clung about St. Francis always; a kind of tack that looked like luck, because it was as simple and direct as a thunderbolt." Thus the Third Order was created. It spread throughout the cities of Italy.

Richard Whitwell quotes from the story of Bl. Lucchesio and describes a "Penitent" or member of the Third Order: "He was a native of Tuscany, but left the little city where he dwelt for political reasons and established himself at Poggio Bonsi near to Siena, where he traded in grain. He became very rich and at one time seems to have made a corner in wheat, buying up all there was and selling it in a time of scarcity, making an enormous profit. But converted by Francis's preaching, he took himself to task, so that his manner of living completely changed. He distributed most of his substance to the poor, merely retaining his house with a garden of four acres, and one ass."

Thuringia's Saint Elizabeth was a Tertiary. On her husband's death she surrendered her royalty, "in order that she might give herself in service to the poor, living like them in a simple way, and working with her hands."

That is how the Third Order worked. Can it work today? And can it work so effectively that it will solve the great dilemma? Well, what is at the heart of the dilemma? It is that we are bound hand and foot to the idea that we must possess material goods if we are to be happy. The dispute between capitalist and socialist loses its sharpness when we reflect that both want more material things. Neither denies the blessing of having more; their only quarrel is as to how goods shall be distributed. St. Francis never surrendered his original ideal of holy Poverty. In founding the Third Order he merely substituted another term. Instead of Poverty he used the term Stewardship.

But to accept stewardship as a substitute for absolute ownership necessitates a change of heart, of mind, of will. It is a revolutionary change. G. K. Chesterton wrote of distributism, men today talk of private enterprise or nationalization, but the hunger to have and to hold is still there. Mankind's spirit must be freed from this obsession which works the world so much ill. To the Franciscan there is no such thing as private property—nobody owns anything—in the sense of being free to do what he would with it. All we have or hold belongs to God and we are the stewards of it. To be stewards of it, preserves man's freedom of soul. G. K. Chesterton believed in distributism (everybody owning something), because he believed that you could not possess the virtues of stewardship unless you had something to be steward over. But when private property and national property are regarded as God's property and men only stewards of it, then we have resolved the bitter dialectic of the economics of today. Perhaps many fear it is easier for a private individual to act as a steward to property than for the State to experience a change of heart. God may speak direct to an individual, but who can convert a State? That question need not be answered now. It is the principle that matters.

The saint was inspired to anticipate the principles of the most significant utterances of modern times, the *Rerum Novarum* of Pope Leo XIII, "the workers' charter." The family was still the basic unit, and "blessed are the horny hands of toil." Individualism and collectivism are not to knock their heads together forever in head-on collision. They are to be transcended by the gospel of love, the doctrine of equality before God, of brotherhood in Christ, of the dignity of man and of labor. Penury is not poverty, slums are not kindergartens for Heaven, unemployment is not anticipatory of eternal rest, property is not to be defended by wolves' fangs, money is not a weapon against communal good. "All that I have and hold I owe to your loving kindness; therefore I restore it to you and make it over (trado) to the utter dominance of your will." That is the majestic Jesuit prayer, that is the spirit of *Rerum Novarum,* and that was the inspiration of the Third Order. Property, governance of industry, craftsmanship? Hold it for Christ! That is Franciscan stewardship.

But can it work? Are men capable of effecting

such a radical change of values? Is it not against the grain of human nature? The answer is given by St. Peter, by St. Paul, by St. Francis himself; by David Livingstone, Father Damien, John Wesley, Florence Nightingale. The answer is given by that great army in every age whose hearts have been changed by the supernatural grace of God—by every saint, by every hero of spiritual adventure, by every drunkard made sober, by every sensualist made pure, by the millions of the selfish who were converted to the compassion of God! The answer is given by the thunder of millions of voices from Heaven, where the redeemed dwell. The answer is given in a multitude of homes, by saintly mothers and good fathers. Society today is permeated by scientists, artists, writers, lawyers, accountants, doctors, business men and industrial leaders, black-coated workers, and those who work with their hands—all of whom are members of the Third Order.

In an eloquent passage Chesterton wrote:

"That morning glory which St. Francis spread over earth and sky has lingered as a secret sunshine under a multitude of roofs and in a multitude of homes. In societies like ours nothing is known of such a Franciscan following. Nothing is known of such obscure followers; and if possible less is known of the well known followers. If we imagine passing us in the street a pageant of the Third Order of St. Francis, the famous figures would surprise us more than the strange ones. For us it would be like the unmasking of some mighty secret society."

Can it work? It does work! Let us subject the problem to some basic thinking.

CHAPTER 5

Practical Program of the Third Order

DEFINITIONS:

What precisely is Poverty in the Franciscan sense?

At root it is not concerned with the plentitude or the lack of material goods. It is rather a spiritual change in our attitude toward possessions. Our Savior was the Divine Reason, so that there must have been good reason in his placing "poverty of spirit" among the Eight Beatitudes. And so we start in a very practical way. We start by *disciplining* the human instinct which wants to accumulate (grab?) property, to enjoy it (self-indulgence, self-pride?), and to guard it (like a dog with a bone?), or just to hoard it and gloat over it (like a miser). That is it—we are to begin by subjecting our instinctive desire to have and to hold property to a stern discipline.

Why not? Civilized man has had to learn to discipline lust and to transmute it into the sanctity of wedded life; he has had to discipline his rage that he may not kill; he has been forced to discipline his urge for revenge, lest he render the law of no effect. In a thousand ways a man is subject to discipline from the day he was born. The student disciplines himself for the sake of learning, the athlete for the sake of physical fitness.

Then why should not this mighty urge to gain and enjoy property be disciplined? For it is not an innocent desire! A vast and terrible sum of evil flows from that undisciplined desire, lying, cheatery, robbery, inflicting penury and sorrow on others, luxury and vice and the wielding of the grossest power ever wielded by man—the power of money. The misery and ruin wrought by this uncontrolled lust for goods cries aloud to Heaven, and the State by a thousand laws strives to curb this lust.

It is, therefore, demonstrated beyond cavil that the instinct to acquire wealth is one that civilized peoples are compelled to restrain. But who is to exercise restraint—the State or the individual?

If restraint were exercised by the State alone, then man's lust for wealth would still remain unstemmed. All statutes have their loopholes; the ingenuity of the cunning mind is the more challenged to cheat the laws. Corruption in high places, robbery in low places, wholesale evasion of those laws designed to ensure an equitable distribution of good (for instance as in Britain), all point to failure. The lust for wealth, gotten well or ill gotten, is like a head of water trying to find the lowest level, it seeps through every chink in the dam and undermines all barricades.

The inevitable conclusion is that the only effective restraint on the lust for wealth is that exercised by the individual himself by his own conscious volition and by the grace of God. What is demonstrated is that this is the only hope for disciplining an instinct which corrupts the soul of man. The Franciscan way of discipline is thus proved to be the only effective and practical way.

But it is not only the possession of money that is significant; there is also the manner in which a man enjoys his wealth even when it is acquired lawfully. Luxury that goes beyond reason, debauchery that feeds the bestial appetites, the use of money power to enslave or degrade others or to gain corrupting adulation—these evil manifestations can hardly be checked by laws. When the question of the right use of wealth arises, then it is all the more certain that the only salvation is by a change of heart in the individual, by the grace of God, as St. Francis taught by word and example.

THREE COROLLARIES:

There are three corollaries to be drawn from the foregoing argument.

1. First, that men and women for the sake of the common good and the glory of God, must forego

the opportunity to amass money—instances are those scientists who devote their lives to research into the cause and cure, let us say, of tropical diseases, and by selfless labor forego monetary emoluments and die in poverty; and those religious in convents who dedicate their worldly goods to God and their neighbor by sacred vows.

2. A second corollary is that one curbs the instinct at its very source by refusing to make money dishonestly or by taking advantage of weaker people. Men who made this great refusal in obedience to what is called commercial morality constitute the salt that keeps commerce healthy or even makes it possible. All commerce is based on the belief that the majority of those engaged in it are honest in word, deed and bond. But the minority grow rich.

3. A third corollary is that we may not support systems of commerce or industry which rate profits above the well-being of the workers. In the old days there was criminal callousness regarding processes (lead poisoning, silicosis, tuberculosis, etc.) which endangered health. That has largely been taken care of by legislation, but the principle is true that an industry must be judged by the kind of men it produces, not by the profits it makes.

Let there be no silly sentimentalism about profits. By and large the chief test of the efficiency of an industry is that it makes a profit. Bankruptcy is not necessarily a proof of righteousness. It is the duty of a Christian man to succeed in any undertaking in which he is a leader. Weaklings have ascribed their failure to their righteousness; mostly it is the result of their inefficiency. The supreme triumph is when a business or industrial corporation is not only a financial success but allocates a just reward to its employees. Nothing hard and fast can be laid down, but the reward must be something that goes one better than what one is compelled to give. A Franciscan will take pride in the happiness and prosperity and the truest well-being of those who cooperate with him by their labor. The Franciscan worker will, of course, give his utmost in return for his wage—and more than that, will take pride in his work as service done not only to his employer but to God and his fellow men. When St. Paul sent Onesimus, the runaway slave, back to his master Philemon, he did not relieve him of the duty of service but he bade Philemon treat Onesimus as a brother in Christ.

That raises a question which constitutes the dilemma of modern industry, namely, the question of the influence of mass production, its monotonous repetitive processes on the moral nature of the worker. All we can say here is that the Christian industrial leader must bend his mind to this problem and never acquiesce in any system however (apparently) necessary which may have ill effects on the worker. We must eliminate the word "impossible" from the realm of industrial relationships. What is right, must be possible in a world governed by God. The problem can only be solved by men of the best brains who have submitted themselves to God's will.

STANDARD OF LIVING:

So there we have it: discipline in every aspect of the possession and use of material goods. For instance, there is the big question of what standard of living we shall maintain. If we aim at a standard of living and a status in society which so strains our financial resources that it stultifies all desire to devote money to good causes, and causes us fret and fever of mind, this must be wrong indeed.

There is a story extant somewhere in America which pictures a community the citizens of which are content with their simple way of life. Then Mary comes home. Mary has been "getting around" and has made good and has become sophisticated. She aims to be the leader of the smart set. After the first feeble effort of resistance by the women of the town, the insidious ambition begins to work. At first smarter clothing, then bigger parties, then better houses, then bigger cars. Expenditure goes up while bitterness and jealousy and envy increase. The men are frantic. Everybody is trying "hell for leather" to keep up with Mary.

One forgets the end of the story. One imagines

that the bubble burst—the whole town found relief in bankruptcy, and after Mary's departure man and wife settled down to the happiness of simplicity of life. But is not that a true parable? Is not mean social ambition creating spiritual misery? Is that the way to use money? No, once more we say how reasonable and practical the Franciscan way is. "Temperance" is a word that has become narrowed to the sphere of drinking, but its true definition is that of a lovely Christian virtue. It strives for the fine fastidiousness which practices moderation not out of meanness, but out of a sense of the sacred character of our true self, which need never be glutted, which must never go too far or take too much, and expresses the soul of a man who stands loose from all material things lest he be enmeshed by the desire of the eyes and the lust of the flesh and by envy and pride. The editor of *Punch* once described the Scots people as "the happy mean." Scotsmen smiled at the double intention. But may we not say that the Christian does in reality belong to the happy mean? Not too much!

DANGER OF MISCONCEPTION:

But there is a danger that the impression has been conveyed that the Third Order program can be taken in bits and pieces. It is profounder than that—in all the profundity of utter simplicity.

The implications and corollaries of the Third Order

argument flow from one unified source. St. Francis did not start by giving up his place in a rich father's house and then go on to one step after the other as opportunity arose. His whole life was a unity. His initial renunciation and the final consummation of the Stigmata were one—one integral decision. Everything was the logical unfolding of his act of faith when he gave himself to Christ and to holy Poverty.

All that has been written in this chapter will flow naturally from one decision—to give all to Christ. The Christian is no opportunist. He acts once and for all.

YET—DOES IT WORK?

All things work together for good when a man has a living relationship with God through Jesus Christ. All these ideals of which we have written—if we attempt to realize them by our own strength we shall be trying merely to lift ourselves by our own waist-belt. The way of life we have envisaged is God's will and, therefore, will be implemented by God's power. When we ask "Can it work?", we reckon without the grace of the Lord Jesus Christ. Once the initial act of faith is made their will be struggles but always the assurance of victory. The Third Order asks nothing impossible, because nothing is impossible to God.

It is precisely because humanitarians omit God

from their plans to ameliorate the misery of mankind that they fail so dismally. Let us look at the United Nations Organization. We speak with respect, for some good must emerge from sincere attempts to come together and take counsel. But we fear it may allay symptoms without curing mankind's desperate disease. U.N.O., alas! does not possess fundamental unity of spirit. It is constituted of individuals not yet fused by a single faith. It has some members who owe no allegiance to the Lord Jesus Christ. How can a body so fundamentally disunited do more than ameliorate surface conditions?

Somebody has boasted that U.N.O. will introduce a golden age comparable to the days of Charlemagne. A good example of the fallacy that blinds men who have no more than humanitarian sentimentality! For in the days of Charlemagne men lived in the unity of one faith in a Church not yet rent in twain by individualism and nationalism. Today that fundamental condition is missing. Civilization is not fused by faith in one God, one Savior.

We must forget councils, however august, forget even the State, when it comes to salvation from sin. We must begin with ourselves. In the soul of a single man all revelations and revolutions begin. This is a matter between us and God. We and God are face to face. He asks for all, that he may give all. In humble penitence and prayer we must throw ourselves at his feet, and he will raise us up and bless us beyond dreaming. When we know for sure that all earthly goods and all the glittering prizes of the world will dissolve into dust, then the certainty of immortality with God will be ours. For the prize of the high calling that is set before us let us run the race.

Another "But"

After that confident and ringing assertion it seems a pity that a "but" should follow. But without it we may visualize ourselves as lonely soldiers fighting as free lances against the solid phalanx of the world. The opposite is the glorious truth. The man who belongs to the Lord Christ, is surrounded by a great cloud of witnesses, great allies stand shoulder to shoulder with him, the Church Victorious in Heaven is with him, the saints uphold him.

"I have a Captain, and the heart
    Of every private man
Has drunk the valor from his eyes
    Since first the war began;
He is most merciful in fight,
    And of his scars a single sight
The embers of our failing might
    Into a flame can fan."

You see, the Christian man belongs to Christ's Church, which is His body. Our Lord founded the

Church so that his disciples should be constantly sustained and trained by living communion with him. St. Francis found this from the very beginning. He clung to the sacraments and the authority of the Church as the very condition of his life. He knew that as a free lance he would fail and all that he did run into the sand. The Church conserved his message even as the banks of the river conserve the life giving waters which because of the sustenance and discipline flow at last triumphantly into the Eternal Sea. And so the Christian lives within Christ's Church.

CHAPTER 6

Nothing Impossible to the Church

THE TRAGEDY of the dreamer throughout the ages has been his loneliness. William Morris echoed his lament:

"Dreamer of dreams, born out of my due time,
Why should I strive to set the crooked straight?"

The dreamer is obsessed by the feeling of loneliness amid a mocking world. A dream, to come true, must gather to itself men who believe in it. A dream is for comradeship, not for solitude. If men stand aloof, the dream falls with a broken wing and the dreamer dies of a broken heart. Actually that has happened with many artists. That is why so many have segregated themselves from human life; "the world forgetting, by the world forgot." Their minds grew warped, their bright day was done, and they were for the dark. But it is also true of the ordinary man. He is pathetically dependent on being in harmony with society around. It is herd instinct, if you like; but it is in reality comrade instinct. When in loneliness he stands facing the herd, his heart fails him. With no sustaining supernatural grace and no cloud of witnesses to cheer him, he grows tired of his dream of good. He grows bitter. He demands: "Why should I strive to set the crooked straight?"

Therein lies the strength of the Third Order of St. Francis. It was born in the great comradeship of the Holy Catholic Church, and it set men amid a great company. It draws strength from God and from fellow believers. A man may accord intellectual assent to the apostolate of the Third Order; he may believe that he should transmute selfish ownership of good into stewardship accountable to God; he may long to give himself in brotherhood to his fellow men; but if he stands alone, the world breaks him at last. In the end he sighs and says, "It is only a dream. It will not work!"

Of course it will not work! The apostolate of the Third Order assumes life within a Church, assumes an inspiring fellowship, assumes guidance and discipline. In short, it assumes the Church Militant with its living Lord and its saving sacraments and its sustaining faith. It is the Church Militant on earth which looks to the Church Triumphant in Heaven.

Notice this: our first thought of a saint is that he is a dreamer and a mystic. Of course he is; than St. Francis none more so. But our second thought is, what practical men and women they were, what doers of deeds, what efficient manipulators of recalcitrant material! Take St. Clare whom St. Francis called when she was a fair aristocratic girl—Clare of the golden hair. Had she not answered the call of St. Francis on that wild moonlight night of the elopement of her soul, she would have become the spoiled dilettante of good works, fussy about the punctilios of moral life, pottering among the lilies of a pious, even sanctimonious life. But when her shorn hair fell before the altar of God, all her girlhood's vitality and enthusiasm was disciplined to practical work. She, with St. Francis, founded the Order of Poor Clares and the Christlike compassion of the First Order glowed in the Second Order. Her life of toil and travel and administration almost equaled that of St. Francis. Her dreams and prayers gave her the fragrance of sanctity, but the discipline of her new life made her one of the great practical saints whose work has survived the shocks of history and stands today.

Or take St. Francis himself. This golden youth and leader of the bright young things of Assisi, with his charm and camaraderie and his ballads of chivalrous love, might well have achieved an applauded conversion; he might well have indulged in popular slumming, the eloquent and charming head of an eccentric and therefore popular sect. In fact he would have become what sentimentalists such as Sabatier would have us believe he actually was—poet and dreamer and charming humanitarian.

But St. Francis was firmly set within the Holy Catholic Church. This meant that he turned dreams into reality by practical action. Instead of composing ballads, he built a church—actually built it, blistering and scarring his white hands by carrying the stones for the walls. Instead of prancing along a primrose path to the sound of flutes, he trod with bare feet the *via dolorosa* of Italy's snows and its rough-hewn paths. Instead of becoming the leader of a coterie, he established and administered an order by his astonishing and enormous labors. A small frail man who preached to birds, but a veritable giant in action! Those who pray most work hardest!

The Church is the Church of practical men. Dreamers of course like St. John of Patmos, mystic naturally, men of prayer of course, but men who are able to do and plan and labor and create. The Church is not called Militant for nothing. That is not a metaphor or just flag-waving to the blare of trumpets—it spells co-operation, discipline, esprit de corps, inspiration, guidance, power. The frustration of loneliness passes away within the Church. Its creed is a bulwark that sustains the mind and gives it a margin for creative labor in dark days as well as in fair. Its sacraments are wells of living water which refresh the weary soldier. Its hierarchy from

Pope to Priest gives a man what practical men desire, namely discipline and orderly progression in a
plan, a certainty of ultimate victory for the cause.

A man without the Church is like a soldier who
takes a gun and goes off sniping at the vast hordes
of the enemy, leaving the Church Militant to deploy
its forces in obedience to the strategy of God.

A member of the Third Order can live only within
the Holy Catholic Church. The man who will not
submit himself to the Church is a sentimentalist. He
does not even interpret the deep desire of humanity.
For in its heart of hearts this restless humanity calls
out for assurance, authority, an unchanging Faith, an
eternal purpose, a victory promised by God. Michael
de la Bedoyere was surely right when he wrote:
"When the world turns again to Christianity for help
and inspiration, it will be moved to do so by the
desire for some fundamental and tried principles, and
that it expects to hear of a hard and costly discipline."

In my youth I studied under a great theologian
whose soaring mind saw the vision of the Holy
Catholic Church but did not live to draw nigh to
it. But by his words he taught me deep truths, as for
instance (he is writing of our Lord):

"Subordination is godlike. He was in the category
of God, but he did not claim the immunities of God.
The Son would not oust the Father. In a word, he
was not inferior to God, but he was subordinate.

Subordination is not inferiority. Oh, if you could but learn that in this your day, how many griefs, heart-burnings, rebuffs, failures, how much soul bitterness it would save you and your posterity! Subordination is *not* inferiority, and it *is* godlike. The principle is imbedded in the very cohesion of the eternal Trinity, and it is inseparable from the unity, fraternity and true equality of men. It is not a mark of inferiority to be subordinate, to have an authority, to obey. It is Divine. To suffer no lord or master—that is Satanic; to discard all control but superior force is the demonic form of sin, which soon passes into the brutal. To have no loyalty is to have no dignity, and in the end no manhood. The end of it is a hard, coarse individualism, a selfishness gradually growing arrogant (if it be not that to begin with), the rupture of family life, filial faith, homely duty, and kindly rule, and the dissolution of all the fine loyalties of the soul for which great men worthily die."

Subordination is not inferiority! That is the answer to the man who holds back from the Church because he shrinks from discipline and authority, because he loves being a free lance and to indulge that kind of license of mind and will which he calls freedom. Or is that too harsh? Yes, there may be those who just weakly desire to have the athlete's prize without the athlete's training and discipline.

Where else is there any hope for him or for humanity?

The Holy Catholic Church throughout the world is resolutely set against all that decries the divinity of man's reason, that degrades the dignity and liberty of man's personality, resolutely set against all tyrannies whether they be of wealth or of power. Where else in the world is there one coherent organized body, fed and animated by the life-blood of Jesus Christ, inspired by the Holy Spirit of God, recruited from men and women of all nations, of every color and clime, a body openly persecuted or secretly feared by the forces of a godless materialism which drugs and enslaves the soul? Dreaded too by the forces of a godless wealth which seeks to enslave men in economic shackles? Where is there any such body as the Holy Catholic Church, the church which was described by our Savior: "Upon this Rock will I build my Church, and the gates of Hell shall not prevail against it." Can the organizers of a materialistic dialectic or the organizers of power through wealth, boast that their system is founded on an eternal rock and that Hell shall not prevail against it? No, because all systems which are not in harmony with the will of God breed revolt in the soul of their slaves. No slave is so sunk that God cannot call him to the glorious freedom of sonship. Thus soulless tyrannies are doomed to defeat. They are unnatural and unreasonable, because they are not set in the holy will of God. St. Francis of Assisi calls you into this Holy Catholic Church.

All through this book I have striven to look into the eyes of St. Francis and to hear his words; whether it be in the psychological studies of Part One or in the character sketches of Part Two or in the deep plunge in Part Three into the ultimate problem for you and me. I have set up my prayer and will, tried to look into his eyes and to listen to his voice. There was a time, not so long ago (alas! the years that the locusts have eaten!) when I believed I could live and work for my dreams in "splendid isolation." The day came when I said with St. Augustine, "Too late have I loved Thee."

Other books have I written but this is the first book I have written in "holy obedience." In its pages I pray you also may look into the eyes of St. Francis of Assisi and hear his voice. By gesture and words he points to the Church as our eternal hope. The great teacher from whom I have just quoted might well have been thinking of the members of the Third Order of St. Francis when he wrote: "And Society will then be dominated, not by spirits whose best life has been spent in the acquisition of things for the lack of which men and brethren round them are dying, but by that unrequited elect, that great unpaid, whose life is a long surrender and whose fate is to be long misunderstood; who do not clamor for their deserts, because the wages of their sin would be death, and also because their faith is that it is a godlier thing to give than to receive; but they empty themselves to make room in themselves and the world for the fulness and glory of God in the cross of Christ the Lord."

Finally, I believe the spirit of St. Francis was with that American unit of the Third Order which at a provincial convention of its members drew up a program of action which concluded with these words:

"We, sons and daughters of the humble St. Francis, believing with St. Francis that human minds and means are as little adequate for the solution of human problems and the cure of human ills as they are for personal salvation:

"Do herewith most solemnly renew our purpose to conciliate upon ourselves and all mankind the grace and blessing of God as indicated in our rule: by lives in keeping with God's pleasure; by the faithful recitation of our daily Office; by the regular and frequent reception of the Sacraments; and above all by daily attendance at the holy sacrifice of the Mass, in which Christ our Savior himself pleads for us with the Precious Blood shed for mankind on Calvary."